Net Work
Selected Writing

SELECTED WRITING
Net Work

Daphne Marlatt

Edited with an Introduction by Fred Wah

published with assistance from the Canada Council and the
Government of British Columbia through the British Columbia
Cultural Fund and the Western Canada Lottery Foundation

Talonbooks   *Talonbooks*
201 1019 East Cordova   *P.O. Box 42720*
Vancouver   *Los Angeles*
British Columbia V6A 1M8   *California 90042*
Canada   *U.S.A.*

This book was typeset by Linda Gilbert, designed by
David Robinson and printed by Friesen for Talonbooks.
PRINTED IN CANADA
First printing: October 1980

Series editor: Karl Siegler

Canadian Cataloguing in Publication Data

   Marlatt, Daphne, 1942 -
     Selected writing

     Bibliography: pp. 141-42
     ISBN 0-88922-175-8

     I. Wah, Fred, 1939 -   II. Title:
   Net work.
   PS8576.A74A6 1980   C818'.5408   C81-091048-9
   PR9199.3.M37A6 1980

Table of Contents

Introduction

I

I'm really given to the sensual. I really delight in that. That's why I can't get absorbed in the zero, in the blank. Language is leafing out, it's everything that is growing that is organisms, that is body. It's a body. I love that phrase, the body of language. And I'm trying to realize its full sensory nature as much as possible. We live in the world. That's my basic assumption. I don't want to get out of this world. I want to learn everything I can about what it is to live in this world, to be mortal, which I take to be in the body. And language, you know, generates itself & it dies, but it's all there in the body, & that's why I love the music. Because the music is the physical quality of language.

Daphne Marlatt in Interview with George Bowering
Open Letter, 4th Series, No. 3, Spring, 1979.

Casting the nets through the body of writing by Daphne Marlatt shows both a writing teeming with life and a writer working so vigorously and finely that she has surfaced as one of the most acute writing intelligences of her generation. Marlatt is a working writer who walks to her studio on Vancouver's Hastings Street nearly every day to work at her novel or poems, to edit her own and others' work, to seriously engage her world through language. This selection, which spans about fifteen years of writing, should be useful as a document

7

to such diligence.

Marlatt was born Daphne Buckle in 1942 in Melbourne, Australia, but spent her early childhood in Penang, a northern Malaysian island in the Indian Ocean. She and her family spent nine months in England saying goodbye to relatives before emigrating to Vancouver in late 1951. Her childhood home in North Vancouver was on the edge of the forest and the first Canadian author she remembers reading was Pauline Johnson. Marlatt's world of childhood imagination in the new land included writing some plays for herself and other children to perform, reading fairy tales, and getting the usual diluted version of Canadian literature at school—Lampman and Bliss Carman. By the time she went to the University of B.C. in 1960, she had acquired a strong poetic responsibility to Vancouver and the West Coast.

The development of Marlatt's writing has its roots in the activities focused around *TISH* in the early sixties in Vancouver. She was not part of the original group (Frank Davey, George Bowering, Fred Wah, David Dawson, Jamie Reid, Lionel Kearns), but she was directly involved with the second wave of writers who continued *TISH* after the Vancouver Poetry Conference in 1963 (Bob Hogg, Dave Cull, Gladys Hindmarch, Peter Auxier, Dan McLeod).

The early 1960's in Vancouver were fermentive years for these writers. *TISH* had developed out of the need of these West Coast writers to feel tangibly involved with others who shared a similar frustration with an inherited academic view towards writing. George Bowering, Lionel Kearns and Frank Davey had made a few attempts to make contact with the Canadian mainstream as it was seen in Louis Dudek's *Delta*. But around 1960, an open letter to the West Coast writers appeared in *Evidence* magazine pointing out that the same generation of eastern Canadian writers felt tied more directly with New York. Davey, Bowering, Wah and the others felt themselves on the fringe and banded together round the idea of a magazine which would involve their particular poetic concerns. Prior to the publication of *TISH*, this took the form of group discussions centred around the newly published *New American Poetry: 1945-1960*, and particularly Charles Olson's essay, "Projective Verse." The *TISH* writers familiarized themselves with the poetics of the so-called "Black Mountain School" of Charles Olson, Robert Creeley, Robert Duncan and Ed Dorn, and by the summer of 1963 and the Vancouver Poetry Conference (with Charles Olson, Robert Duncan, Robert Creeley, Allen Ginsberg, Denise Levertov, Margaret Avison, Philip Whalen) the West Coast had spawned what Raymond Souster two years later anthologized as *New Wave Canada*. Marlatt was involved then and continues to be an important part of this "explosion in Canadian Poetry."[1]

During the summer of 1963, Marlatt wrote a paper for Olson's class at summer school. It was a paper on etymology, the study of the roots of words. She says "that etymology paper really led me into all the writing I would subsequently do . . . it opened up language for me."[2] In another interview she says, "Creeley, Olson, Duncan all talked a lot about language, its roots, the way it moves. I mean, this is so basic that I can't even think of it in terms of 'influence': simply, they opened up the whole activity of writing for me."[3] The most important books for her when she's writing are dictionaries.

As well as the "Black Mountain" poets Marlatt has had other literary enthusiasms. At university, she read D.H. Lawrence, Virginia Woolf and Henry James. She read H.D.'s novel, *Bid Me to Live*, shortly after it appeared as an Evergreen paperback in 1960. Later, in Indiana, she read Louis Zukofsky's collected short poems, *All*, and while she was working on her book *Rings*, Gertrude Stein's *Tender Buttons* was important to her. Her master's thesis was a translation of *Le Parti Pris Des Choses* by the French poet, Francis Ponge, from whom she learned to trust the "semantic thickness" of words and to explore the limits of English syntax. She explains that the contemporaries she is interested in are "writers who are pushing at an edge that is going to inform my edge."[4] Of the work of her Canadian contemporaries, she turns most often, lately, to Michael Ondaatje's *Coming Through Slaughter*, George Bowering's *Burning Water* and Robert Kroetsch's *Badlands*, texts which "are very important to me because they move in a direction in prose I want to move in."[5] Similarly in poetry, she feels an affinity with the work of George Bowering, Fred Wah, Michael Ondaatje, Brian Fawcett, bp Nichol and Gerry Gilbert. While she acknowledges a correspondence between the concerns of her own texts and those of her companions, she is quick to point out that, "the dialogue with these people is as primary as the actual books are."[6]

An early novella Marlatt had written in a fiction-writing class she was taking from Earle Birney in 1962 was published in *Evidence* about that time. In an interview in 1976, she said, "That was 'The Sea Haven.' It's my only piece of fiction and I feel rather strange about it. I'd like to pretend it doesn't exist."[7] She also published a few poems in *Raven*, the student literary magazine at U.B.C., and a story in *a concept*, a magazine from the school of architecture. She published just a little with *TISH* (first series) and, in fact, Frank Davey had refused to print some of her work in *TISH*, accusing her of "falling into my imagination and failing to sort of live up to the Williams criteria of literalism, & precision, & accuracy to geography & place."[8]

Marlatt spent the year after the Vancouver Poetry Conference in Vancouver and then moved with her husband, Alan Marlatt, to Bloomington, Indiana in the fall of 1964, after a summer in Spain. As she explains it, she felt "dead-ended" until she began writing *Frames of a Story* (Ryerson, 1968):

> I could not begin *Frames* until I had spent all of the sum-
> mer of '64 in ideal writing circumstances. That is, we were

located in one place on the coast of Spain and I thought, "Great, I can spend the whole summer writing"—and I couldn't write anything. I just was really dead-ended. I went to Bloomington, Indiana that fall with my husband and I was there on no particular visa. I mean, my category there was basically as his wife—I couldn't study, I couldn't get a job—and again, it was ideal for writing and I couldn't write. That Christmas we came up to Canada, to Montréal, and I felt so good about coming back: I'd never realized until that point that I did identify very strongly as a Canadian. And so when I went back to Indiana, I said, "Okay, I'm going to forget about everything I learned in '63 and '62 and I'm going to go back to my own sources" and the earliest sources I had were fairy tales. Of course, reading Duncan allowed me to go back, I mean right back to childhood, because he is constantly stressing the importance of that. So I went to Hans Christian Andersen's fairytale of the Snow Queen and just started from there. This gave me a structure, a story line I didn't have to worry about because it was already "told," so I could then move into the writing out of what was simply coming up each day in the act of writing.[9]

Frames is a poem/story-weaving of psyche and soul. It was an important personal experience for Marlatt to write the book, an affirmation of identity. She doesn't simply use Andersen's story as a "frame" for her own experience, but, by allowing the persona to be revealed through Andersen's characters and events (as the real story is revealed through the telling of it), the writer traverses a personal terrain.

> The real story is about being lost. Kay is lost, but Gerda's lost, too. Every step of the way she's lost. She has no idea how it's going to end. She doesn't know how she's going to get from the place she starts out, with her intention, which is of finding Kay & bringing him back to life. She has no idea how that will be accomplisht. Everything happens along the way. That was my first image of process, of just going, of telling a story.[10]

While writing *Frames* in Bloomington in 1965 and 1966, Marlatt met D. Alexander, a young poet and linguist who helped her listen more closely to her natural speech patterns and tighten up her line. Her next book, *leaf leaf/s* (Black Sparrow, 1969), dedicated to D. Alexander, is the result of a sharp, technical focus on language. The poems in *leaf leaf/s* show also an imprint from her reading of Louis

Zukofsy in their slightly whimsical play with sound and syntax. The content of the poems is highly personal and referentially obscure. She points out to Bowering that at the time she wasn't primarily interested in content and that in *leaf leaf/s* she still finds the "sparseness of the language . . . a challenge."[11]

By 1969, when *leaf leaf/s* was published, Marlatt had gained a particular awareness of her own writing possibilities. In response to a question about the different poetic style of her book *Rings* (Georgia Straight Writing Supplement, 1971), she explains her alternatives:

> Well, *leaf leaf/s* was really a poetic apprenticeship for me. It was the sharpening of my ear. . . . But I had begun basically with prose. In fact, *Frames* was originally entirely written in prose, and after *leaf leaf/s*, I felt too confined by the short line and by absolute attention at every step to the word, so I decided to open up the line deliberately and to use that extended line which looks like prose—left margin to right margin on the page. Compared to verse, it's an approximation of a line because internal punctuation is just as important. And the paragraph breaks are very important. Like, I wanted to move in larger units, in paragraphs, and I wanted larger rhythms than those very short lines would allow.[12]

Rings is a long prose-poem in six sections. Once again, the content is specific and personal and the process of writing the book for Marlatt was revelatory and informative. "The first section was written precisely at the time that it was being written about, at the time of the time that was being written about . . . charting a territory that was unknown, that I found myself in & having to map it out in order to discover where I was—i.e., what's going on here."[13] The book documents the strain of a distintegrating marriage and the birth of a first child. The writer's perspective in this book is an interesting one. As also, in a beautiful recent piece called "Listen," here Marlatt is able to give a depth to the narrative by the particular action of "voice," an attractive benefit of her style of writing. This is what has been termed the "middle voice," a voice that is between the active and the passive and denotes "action done for oneself."[14] It is a difficult "voice" to achieve in English, but Marlatt seems to have mastered it.

> Marlatt's approach is again thoroughly phenomenological: every image and reflection of the woman's multiphasic consciousness is recorded—some by means of puns, metaphors, split words, parenthetical phrases. Fragmented

11

syntactic structures free the reader to slow his pace and re-live the woman's experiences at the same rate that they have exploded upon her senses. The resultant linguistic structure is one of the most beautiful in our literature.[15]

Two of Marlatt's major works, *Vancouver Poems* and *Steveston*, reveal a concern she shares with other "new wave" writers with the "local," a sensibility she derives not only from William Carlos Williams' *Paterson* and Charles Olson's *Maximus Poems*, but also from a literal "spiritual resonance"[16] with the West Coast. "I'm interested in the interaction between the eternal & what's time-bound, & what's particularly local. And I think you can only articulate the eternal thru . . . the local & the time-bound. And that's what makes us most human."[17]

Following the publication of *leaf leaf/s*, Marlatt returned to Vancouver for 1968-69, and wrote most of *Vancouver Poems* (Coach House Press, 1972) the following year while living in Wisconsin. The book is generated from Marlatt's need to engage the spirit of "her" place. "Part of it was the fact that, again, I wanted to make Vancouver very real to me."[18] She returned to Vancouver in the summer of 1970, researched old newspaper clippings and pamphlets in the Vancouver Public Library and acquainted herself with some of the basics of Northwest Coast Indian mythology in order to write the poems.

Vancouver Poems "began as whole fragments excised from the writing of *Frames*"[19] and the book is initialized by Marlatt's need to portray the mythologies of people she knew and remembered as well as the mythology of the place. Speaking of the sequence of the poems, she says:

> It's as if I was drilling, like thru the present—& the immediate present was the people that I knew—down from that into a larger collective present, which was the streets, the city, things I was seeing on the streets, like the English Bay poem; down deeper into, quote, history, the fire & so on ; deeper still, prehistory, which was before the written records that we keep, native Indian.[20]

By the time she was writing *Vancouver Poems*, she was able to take far greater risks in her play with the wide range of line, syntax, rhythm and rhyme at which she had become adept. A poem like "Alcazar, Cecil, Belmont, New Fountain, names" is one of the most powerful and artistic utterances of poetic historiography in Canadian writing.

Marlatt returned to Vancouver again in 1971 and has resided there since. Soon after returning to the West Coast, she became involved in an oral-history project at U.B.C. which, for her, resulted in her major work of the seventies, *Steveston*. The book was published in 1974 with Robert Minden's powerful black & white photographs paralleling the intense prose-poem. The sequence verifies her consistently "prioprio-ceptive" stance towards her materials: the terrain around the mouth of the Fraser River, the fish, fishing and economics thereof, the exploi-tation of ethnic groups, particularly the Japanese-Canadian, and of the destitute and of the female. "History in these poems becomes both personal and contemporary; the 'political' implications of the facts Marlatt discovers reach into both her life and the reader's."[21] The experience of writing *Steveston* brought Marlatt to a mature conscious-ness about the responsibility of her writing and language.

> I take it that a writer's job is to continue to give accurate witness of what's happening. One person isn't going to change what Marathon Realty is doing, what the CPR is doing. . . . You cannot change the world. You can change consciousness, & language is intimately tied up with con-sciousness. That's our true field of action, is language, as poets. And all you can do is to insist on the seeing as it's evidenced & manifested in the language. In an accurate use of language.[22]

And the language of *Steveston* is a gain in confidence and authority, while not losing the engaging step-by-step intricacies of particular attention to the writing process Marlatt has become recognized for.

While working on the Steveston oral-history project, Marlatt also worked at a sequence of short pieces which relate to a year she spent in a communal living situation in Vancouver. The five narratives, dated 1972-73, were published as *Our Lives* (Truck Press, 1975). The collection is a delightful, careful articulation of the writer's "psyche" in passage to the world of the "ethos," the house, the daily house. The same attention to detail as in her poetry occurs in this long line which reads like prose. In fact, through most of Marlatt's writing, the reader will undoubtedly experience some difficulty in distinguishing between the prose and the poetry.

> My notion re prose & poetry is that I'm confused. I have a feeling that both of them have nothing to do with the way they look on the page, but with the way the language is moving. A particular kind of attention to language. Simply, that standard prose is written as if language was transpar-ent. You're not seeing it. Poetry is written with the aware-ness that it's not transparent, that it is in fact a medium, & that you are operating in it thanks to it. It's like the difference between being land animals &—we don't usually experience air, you know. We breathe in & we breathe out without being aware that we're breathing in any medium at all. That it is our medium. Once we get

into the water, which is a foreign element to us, we're very aware of the difficulty of moving thru that element. That's like poetry. You are aware that you are moving in an element, in a medium, & that there is a constant resistance to your moving forward. And that, in fact, any moving forward you make is thanks to that element that you're moving in. So that language . . . writes the story as much as you do.[23]

Marlatt's first complete book of prose, *Zócalo* (Coach House Press, 1977), does seem more accessible as "prose." The cover notes explain it is: "A travel book about getting lost. A sequence of days and nights in the Yucatan. A Canadian couple, a woman travelling with her lover Yoshio. Lost in the square, the zócalo, in the centre of town, reading a dream, reading the way the actual light falls—Mexico lies all around them." *Zócalo* is a sensuous journal-novel which, like *Frames*, charts perception after perception, looking to find a way. "Entering unknown territory, where you always find out a lot about yourself, your strengths and fears . . . you're fixed on that gridiron of those strengths and fears . . . the mapmaking ends up being a map of those."[24]

At present, Marlatt is at work on a novel and for the past few years she has edited (with Paul de Barros) a prose magazine, *periodics*. She seems committed to continued exploration in prose. "I mean, even the word 'story' sets up a CLANG in my body, it just pulls me so much."[25] The reader can be sure of movement at the frontier, of a view of the horizon.

II

Put yourself inside the head of a bird as he's flying down a channel of water. Okay. Now the image would be what you see if you're outside on the bank looking up at him. That's not what I'm interested in. I'm interested in getting you inside his head in flight. And everything's moving. There is no still reference point because he's in flight, you're in flight. Whoever's reading.

Daphne Marlatt in Interview with George Bowering
Open Letter, 4th Series, No. 3, Spring, 1979.

Lost on a journey, travelling through unknown territory, dependent on self resource, the metaphor is nearly too simple. The condition of being lost suggests one does not know where one is in relation to some larger image, or that one doesn't know where the journey will end. There are dangers and pitfalls, the adrenalin flows, the energy level is intense. Frequently, Marlatt's readers also feel lost in the writing;

there seems no message, no direction, the language isn't operating the way we expect. Yet within this bewilderment and apprehension discovery and revelation can be found. The problem has to do, in Marlatt's case, with where her language comes from. She strives for a writing which will accurately reflect the condition of the writer at the moment of the writing. This is called "proprioceptive" writing and Marlatt is one of its most disciplined proponents.

Proprioception is a physiological term and has to do with the sensory reception in our bodies responding to stimuli arising from within. The term is also the title of a short "chart" written by Charles Olson, circa 1959, in which Olson seeks to place "consciousness," a very important condition for Marlatt. Olson says the gain for proprioception is:

> that *movement* or *action*
> is 'home.' Neither of the Unconscious nor Projection
> (here used to remove the false opposition of
> 'Conscious'; 'consciousness' is self) have a home
> unless the DEPTH implicit is physical being—
> built-in space-time specifics, and moving (by
> movement of 'its own')—is asserted, or found-
> out as such. Thus the advantage of the value
> 'proprioception.' As such.[26]

The "soul" is in the "body." George Bowering's outstanding interview with Daphne Marlatt, quoted in this introduction so extensively, is called "Given This Body." Repeatedly in the interview and elsewhere, Marlatt has insisted on the place of the body in the origins and processes of her writing. When I talked with her recently she said, "I realize things about my living when I'm writing that I think it's necessary for me to realize and I don't seem to be able to realize them any other way."[27] The writing and the living come from within and, consequently, Marlatt insists, so must the reading.

Marlatt's writing is based on a response, literally, to her own consciousness (in the body) as she writes rather than to an outside (projection) more commonly recognizable use of language as reference, as the means by which the world is referred to. When she explained to me how reading D.H. Lawrence in the early sixties had made her realize how it was possible to write about consciousness rather than plot, she defined consciousness as "thinking about thinking; thinking about sensing and perceiving and feeling."[28] In an earlier interview she said, "I think that consciousness is simply part of the recognition of our existing, that our existing is an activity that is carried on instant by instant, moment by moment, and that to be here, to really be here, we have to be aware of that, of all of it."[29] The language in such an attentive kind of writing is necessarily immediate and precise and it is

15

worth considering the specific qualities therein.

> GB: It doubles back on itself & it makes observations on its own language. That makes it difficult to follow for somebody who's for the first time coming on to this kind of verse. Often the reader has to zero in on the words rather than on what they refer to.
> DM: Yes. I mean it's literally step-by-step, word-by-word. Because, if you're lost, the only reference point you have is yourself, right? So you just keep going.[30]

The primary sense of Marlatt's writing is that the reader is in the presence of the making of it. Words, lines, books, chunks of language, pieces, collide in a precision of wordcraft to reveal a poem or story happening right now, right here. I want to stress the value of this kind of writing; it evokes what she has called "the active intelligence in language."[31]

For Marlatt, the "word" is a place to focus the energy of the intelligence, not simply a sign for some other content. In talking to her about *Vancouver Poems*, George Bowering expresses a concern about the maxtrix of the poem and she answers him with a suitably proprioceptive qualification:

> Any word is a physical body. Its body is sound, so it has that absolute literal quality that sound has, which connects it up with sounds around it. And then, it has that other aspect, which is meaning. . . . You move out from the word to a shape, which is the whole poem.[32]

In the poem, "Who could know," the word "wait" floats out there on the page with all that space around it, some kind of mast, signal.

                                                    orchids
flown in crates, "shipments" (Yokohama, Hong Kong,
Shanghai)

          wait

Viaduct. led West, or turning, shadows do in 'gateway
to the east' of rising sun, set, in their sunset.

Or, in "Seeing your world from the outside," a recent poem, what stands out is how the words' sound-rhyme overlaps with the words' meaning-rhyme ("night," "light," "white," "right" and "write"). This poem is a paradigm of attentiveness, the writer taking care in the language, at work in it. When she breaks the word and line,

16

                    i-
        dentify

we can recognize more of the particularity of the word itself, of its
presence and prescience than we normally do. In other words, by
drawing graphic attention to the word, Marlatt directs the reader to the
initial sound and to the double sound/meaning rhyme of "i" and "I,"
where we discover the meaning of the word embedded in the word
itself.

    Marlatt moves ahead, one word after another, and to do that the
word must be kept open to the mind for a wide range of possibility.
See in the following example how intricate the sound, rhythm and
meaning interweave to push the language forward so that the impact
is a build-up, a construct:

        unspoken his
        head of
        stars stares
        a head

This is not simply "word-play." It is the necessary activity of the
writer's sensory perception responding to the stimuli from the mind
and the body which has interacted with the medium in order to dis-
cover, to locate, and so, to take the next step.

        Well, it's like walking, you know. This kind of writing
        involves thinking aloud, thinking aloud enough to write
        it on the page, to get it from here to there. And that
        art goes thru language. Okay, so I'm walking. I'm walk-
        ing thru one perception or one observation or one idea,
        to the next. And sometimes those ideas, the way they
        relate to each other, is a gift. I suddenly see it halfway
        thru the sentence."[33]

Even in some of her syntax involving a longer line Marlatt exercises a
sharp ear to step from one word to the next, tone leading to meaning,
body-sound leading to mind-image-idea:

                                        . . . I imagine the yellow
        eyes of a cavernous head we ourselves have filled with light. Night . . .

This writing depends on itself, moves on its own steam, instant by
instant, ahead. In the following example from *Steveston*, a word grows
and repeats to set up the larger syntactic rhythm:

                            17

no more than the requisite, *required* to grow, spawn
catch, die: required to eat.

The word is a place to come to and leave from, signalling changes in
direction. The word "lurks" acts as a transmission for the movement
of the main images in the opening piece from *Steveston*, which starts
with "town" and ends with "fish." She constantly pushes at the bound-
aries of the word-world.

This intense, particular care with the word, in fact, creates, by its
nature, a larger concern. In Marlatt's writing, the transforming words
set up the line as the basic rhythmic unit. The precision she gives to
the line as a unit of measure, through all her work, indicates one of
the most attentive ears in writing today. Functionally, the line is the
measure of the "breath" in her writing (enforced by her recognition
of Pound's "musical phrase" and Olson's "HEART, by way of the
BREATH, to the LINE"), part of the proprioceptive mechanism. Par-
ticularly in the early poems, she works the line into tight, quick,
syncopated units:

> to/
> go pick black
> berries & raz
> berries,
>   she sd the
> contact high in
> vites rambles well

The way she breaks the words and lines here is not arbitrary. The body
process pays attention to and informs a particular rhythm, a way of
saying it (as opposed to other ways of saying those words together).
This is what dominates the fragment, more than "what" is being said.

The range of Marlatt's ability with the line is fully realized in *Van-
couver Poems*, where the poems tax the space of the page congruent
with the variety of statement she explores. Throughout the poems,
we see, literally, if they are read aloud, the use of the line as dance, as
step; single-word lines shift into longer lines and swirl off into stanzas
and stanzagraphs and return. This movement back and forth is the
prosus and versus of the Greek chorus and it confounds those describers
who are concerned to label her writing prose or verse.

In a short essay she wrote recently for *Open Letter* titled "The
measure of the sentence,"[34] Marlatt explains her sense of how the line
operates in her own writing:

> At that time (1970) i was still writing shortline poems
> concomittant with the longline ones, but it was the latter,
> which i thought of as "prose poems," that engaged me

most, most gave me room to play around. I wanted to build syntactic structures that i could sustain far longer than i could in verse, & i wanted to build looser & more complicated rhythms. It wasn't just a case of extending my lines. I had to really believe i was writing prose, tho with a poet's ear on the pulse of the language.

She explains that she had written *Rings* this way, "thinking i was writing prose," but when it came time to set the type for publication she realized "there was in fact a functional right margin. Where the line of words broke on the page, that edge functioned as a hesitation, sounded a rhythmic break only slightly less insistent than a period or comma." So the line, like the word, functions for her as a unit in the writing with similar generative possibilities. In the same essay, she says:

> I had definitely abandoned the textbook notion of sentence
> as the container for a completed thought, just as writing
> open form poetry had taught me the line has no box for a
> certain measure of words, but a moving step in the process
> of thinking/feeling, feeling/thinking." Our word "sentence"
> comes from L. *sentire*, to feel, think—the muscularity, the
> play of thought that feels its way, flexive and reflexive,
> inside the body of language. In short, a proprioceptive
> (receiving itself) prose.

The body can feel the rhythm and the intelligence behind it, the lines as breaths. When Marlatt sets the prose line in *Zócalo*, she refuses to abandon this concern with rhythm to convention, but rather she plays off that convention by her insistence that the sentence continue to hold the (its) breath. The intense rhythmic syntaxes are determined by units of breathing the language:

> their old trunks' tatter whitewash adrift in peels, the
> balloon man goes slowly by, trailing pinks & blues through
> a trickle of hose . . .

The phrase becomes the breath measure and we are drawn to that in the way the phrases insist on their own length, insist on being spoken that way. In other words, she is maintaining her control over the "line" unit in prose by enforcing it in or juxtaposing it with the grammatical "phrase."

In her poem *Steveston*, she explores and plays in the landscape that the turns of syntax make, and this movement *across* the page, across voices, parallels the traversing across the history and imagination of that place at the mouth of the Fraser River, at that place on the tongue of the writer.

Shadowy, this
piratical emblem of another era. Boomtown. Dream of seizing silver wealth that
swims, & fixing it in solid ground, land, home. A mis-reading of the river's
push. Now Moncton Street walks a straight line that begins & ends. Never a

And finally, there is the "book," the larger of the measurable units
Marlatt works at. As with "word" and "line," "book" for her is a very
intentional form. For this collection, for example, she has rearranged
the selection from *Vancouver Poems*, since out of the context of the
original book the poems suggested to her a different order. The three
different "Stevestons" (these are: *Steveston*, the prose-poem with
Robert Minden's photographs, *Steveston Recollected,* the documen-
tation published by the Provincial Archives, and "Steveston," a C.B.C.
radio playscript adapted by Marlatt from the first two) are interesting
in this regard since each of the three texts she produced out of the
same oral-history project is a base which evokes a different "content"
in her writing, what it is all about at a given point in time and at a given
point in the writing.

I have chosen to direct your attention in this introduction to the
elements of prosody in Marlatt's work because that is what I believe is
most significant about her writing so far. Some readers have difficulty
with the "way" she writes. I believe that difficulty is necessarily part
of the proprioceptive origin and attention of her writing, and, remain-
ing faithful to that tropism, she doesn't have a choice. The reward, of
course, is still the illumination.

The selection of writing here includes pieces from all of Marlatt's
published books to date. The selections from *Rings* and *The Columbus
Poems* are taken from the recently-edited *What Matters: Writing 1968-
70* (scheduled for Coach House Press publication in 1980), as are a
number of other pieces from that period. Besides several previously
unpublished new poems I have also included a few pieces from "In the
Month of Hungry Ghosts," a powerful document of her visit to Penang
in 1976, just published in an exceptionally beautiful issue of *The
Capilano Review*, alongside Michael Ondaatje's journal, "Running in
the Family." There are some worthwhile essays and interviews (notably
Barbour, Davey and Bowering) the student will find useful and which
illustrate aspects of Marlatt's writing I have not noted. It was difficult
to select from her writing and interviews. Her imagination and the
world it works in is lush; a beautiful and very real sense of people and
place, absolutely located in an incredibly powerful poetic intelligence.

Fred Wah,
South Slocan, B.C.
September 1979-September 1980.

Footnotes:

1. Raymond Souster, ed., *New Wave Canada* (Toronto, Contact Press, 1966).
2. A taped conversation between Daphne Marlatt and Fred Wah, South Slocan, B.C., July, 1980.
3. David Arnason, Dennis Cooley and Robert Enright, "There's This and This Connection," *CVII*, Vol. 3, No. 1, Spring, 1977, p. 29.
4. *Op cit.*, Marlatt/Wah.
5. *Ibid.*
6. *Ibid.*
7. *Op. cit.*, Arnason, Cooley and Enright, p. 28.
8. George Bowering, "Given This Body," *Open Letter*, 4th Series, No. 3, Spring, 1979, p. 35.
9. *Op. cit.*, Arnason, Cooley and Enright, p. 29.
10. *Op. cit.*, Bowering, p. 41.
11. *Ibid.*, p. 55.
12. *Op. cit.*, Arnason, Cooley and Enright, p. 29.
13. *Op. cit.*, Bowering, p. 63.
14. Robert Graves and Alan Hodge, *The Reader over Your Shoulder* (New York, Vintage Books, 1979).
15. Frank Davey, *From There to Here* (Erin, Porcépic, 1974), pp. 194-195.
16. *Op. cit.*, Bowering, p. 34.
17. *Ibid.*, p. 58.
18. *Ibid.*, p. 70.
19. *Ibid.*, p. 71.
20. *Ibid.*, p. 72.
21. *Op. cit.*, Davey, p. 195.
22. *Op. cit.*, Bowering, p. 82.
23. *Ibid.*, pp. 61-62.
24. *Op. cit.*, Marlatt/Wah.
25. *Op. cit.*, Bowering, p. 36.
26. Charles Olson, *Additional Prose*, George Butterick, ed. (Bolinas, Four Seasons Foundation, 1974), p. 18.
27. *Op. cit.*, Marlatt/Wah.
28. *Ibid.*
29. *Op. cit.*, Arnason, Cooley and Enright, p. 31.
30. *Op. cit.*, Bowering, p. 42.
31. *Op. cit.*, Marlatt/Wah.
32. *Op. cit.*, Bowering, pp. 69-70.
33. *Ibid.*, p. 61.
34. An essay by Daphne Marlatt written in the Spring of 1980, solicited by Frank Davey, ed., for *Open Letter*.

from FRAMES OF A STORY

I   white as of the white room

Gerda 'n Kay actinic
names that shatter
walls

step into light they leave
this closet to be
open include night
to make out of a lamp
of their names a dark
space

these paper
characters of air?

no, but keep
names' mineral in hand
whose cold burns just
to keep in touch

with how it is to be
this frozen
by your going, you
who actually returned
here, haven't I
slept

your arms in mine, dreamt
not the same
dreams that slip
undeliverable

here
is the real odour of soup
in skinny fingers, onion
of daily accident

O I make soup carefully for you
that we do eat/sleep together yet
these walls refrigerate us

lit with their names
illegibly scrawled defiant or
halfseen murmurs

walls that fixed
your hand, I
couldn't get beyond
the fact

　　your flesh is white
　　fossil
　　touch

mine not
in the swallowed
spaces of the
mirror

　　where her
　　hair comes
　　clear

who operates
at hand's breadth from eyes
projected rooms
all clarity consumed, witch
keeps this room lockt
on the hour

which names my state of containment (not content—where doors
are lockt . . . or more precisely, this room has none. Not now at any
rate. Though walls show light (eggshell thin), where possibility
turns at the outer webs of eyes . . . she looks out from. That's it:
am I seeing things?

　　　　Easy for you to say. It's a matter of energy I always
associate you with. Sun, & that afternoon where things stood green, the
laurel, car itself metalic in your driving it, uphill . . . Gone. As roses etc.
The scrapbook of any 16-year-old. Up to the very door of goodbye.

Rooms & nights now. & nothing is 3-dimensional but stands: a flat
remembrance, echo, or photograph.

& I'm back in the room with the women weaving . . . a shell? of
nostalgia? Or keeping faith?

I can't stand that faded
crepe paper rose, photograph
stuck to a clip of glass
down a street peering over your shoulder
face turned in the surprise of sun
looks very far off
          which is false
you were looking at me when they snapt
the shutter on the street to fasten us
but faceless, as now
faced with the prospect

through the door to where you sit
scrape back your chair for a cigarette
walk to the window watch
the trees waver
one in another watch
rooms to a star
catapult through the upper
section of window
pane

& want to say wait
as a child calls
wait for me

One minute gone when you turn at the fence, before being swept
on, for a last wave. How could I know that, like gravity gone, I was
suddenly released, aimless. How much your hand still weighed on my
hair, or warm under clothes on my skin, pulling me to you, that grip
gone.

And the actual "pictures" of you (what else) fade from sight, eyes'
betrayal yes. But the whole weight of me shifted, changed value in fact.
Without gravity I was absent too. Blown anywhere, clung to any
personplace (for reprieval), had to begin to be a . . . will.

out of cinnamon hearts I wrapt
myself in the cloak
& so stept through into green
tree a willow
hazed like light knifed
into bone creaks

between rocks & tree & fence
in all spaces (things) a green
web separate as hair strands
every good, the princess
glittering shadow of the prince
attacked, dragged
into the cave was changed
by brilliant hullabaloo
spat on her small stone crouched
under the shrunken crown her head

I made into a saucepan lid
a knocker
the handle of a spoon
made her look in the mirror
when the prince arrived I'd
worn her inside out but he
stabbed me
    right
            through the cloak

in a burst of green I croaked
fell among toads
knew beetles crept the grass

my throat's
immense
moment of dirt

when I came back
we all did somehow
foolish
the roof, house
rose up around

with milk in the kitchen
we, relieved
outstared
windows at the willow

Perhaps the trick was that we were always looking for their looking at us, trees etc., as much as that kitchen-chaired audience we tried hard to please (caught up in "the picture of" dancing, conscious our dance was staged with charms, & fixed as the split between us & them,

& by whom?)

That afterwards they should say darling that was wonderful, better than coins in any tambourine, for they judged us as was meant, as we knew they knew more than we did what was going on in that equally other world we aspired to: our mysteries against theirs. So that one day they would say from their kitchen chairs, yes you've made it, you're here.

No, *here's* the lie. Here where I sit waiting, forced, the female, to abide . . .

VII   Out a rose window

Once there was a girl & boy etc. Once roses exfoliate surround them. Thus unpeeled, they stand nude in the luminous centre of themselves. Back to back to the room. Where windowboxes with roses border their image of the world. Sun. Close up enlarges leaves, a luminescence, an underwater sheen. Fills the room, as it had done, through the framework of their window. Eyes. Transparency. How they transfix each other, in each, see the room & themselves contained.

Only one interesting event occurs on their return: they meet the robbergirl, who has freed herself at last. Was out to see, so she said, the wide world. Signpost, had sped Gerda on her way. And this (with only a shadow of you see!) is Kay. Ah! She is happy for them, she smiles over their joined hands & utters the word: "Snip-snap-snurre-basselurre." Sound of connexion breaking (its bas allure). Progressively Kay & Gerda drift further into summer.

To face on the final page. But. The grandmother. Does her voice stop? Singing, the story says, in heavenly sun—a type of angel extending violets, long since dried, to perfume the odour of her family's underwear.

A child prints firmly in red, they lived happily ever afterwards comma to the end of their summer.

And their names stain the page. Saints standing between the eyes &
brain, exempli, crowned with incredible light & everlasting (roses as
poses there).

Here we must step back from the frame, the delicate tracing of willow.
Not to see through glass shades distort.

For a fact, a facet of light this window looks out on. Besides a star—
who is felt there, on steps the other side of the wall, with cigarette.
Studying the night

    "There'll be room. Yes."
    Doors hang askew in their frames & will not close.
    "Too close to the railroad track? Or to the street?"

Open to a concourse of coming & going. Windows. Rattle each time
that wheels go by. The feet . . . Step over her hands, old woman whose
house this is. Painting her floors against their traffic, trying to maintain
colour & wood. & the miracle: she does.

Not snow that counts, turning it upside down & shaking it, glassed in
here, in the light. Not crystal of watches, time—times I don't know
you. Or even what I hold. Last night when you rose, came, we both did,
toward this point in time: I felt the naked structure of your spine
extend (stars, cold), all your vertebrae unfold . . .

                                    Time to give up,
history as his or theirs & even knowing—where they came from, why
they did, who do you love . . . Long hoot of a train echoes into the
walls pursuit. Is crackt already.

And some minutes after: You're sitting on the back steps in the dark
with cigarette, absorbed, watching the shapes of boxcars travel night.
Or I think you do & don't ask, Stars or boxcars? Step out of the
doorway too, step out & sit, down.

from LEAF LEAF/S

blue

bottle I blow
over a mouth
vibrates lip
sounds

     (burr of
      blue

please if I
blow you
might respond

who blows me from
yr lips' air.

for k, d

sun finds you two
curved

shells on our bed
in a deep
white you're tide
carved

only the
hull of your push.

photograph

you sd a stalk I look
like a weed wind blows
thru

    singly
    smokes &
    fumes

green's
unripe a colour but
elemental, grass
easily hugs
ground, that's you

so cocksure

    i

momentum

eventually of stars
runs down
hill,
    the shingle

back't us slippery
feet collide with dry
sky

ii

as simply
spoken out as even
its tongue
licks lights lightens its
hunger hole in
visible over

black water, branches

lie under
lined our
laughter his
half-expected
emergence from

iii

warm to
touch

iv

unspoken his
head of
stars stares
a head

that lie that eyes
suffice

that we shd kiss & make
up he sd before
driving to
sleep.

to, carry thru

i

to /
go pick black
berries & raz
berries,
           she sd the
contact high in
vites rambles well

surround the hot day lilies
trumpets

heat there in her is
in her to black
what's green before the
summer's out

               'a thousand things'
do hairs on each gem
sprout facts the eye
whispers webs or
spectrums which
knit things into light,

tam
bien tambour
               /een a
little drum

ii

refracts a
sleep a dust or
rest a rust or
death a little

well how else
drink?

iii

trumpets as if
pulling on air
light

exhausts the rim
sticks click the
circle is
          weight is
possibility

               taps on thin
membrane, will it
out? quick
          step or
          steps make their
          way felt
                    there
rhythm per
vades in no
straight line waves
circle their act the
exit

          iv

support an internal
tense in terms of
sea
     sound carries
her, her voice the sun's

you moon, delights, waves
goodbye from where she
stands the day
delivers.

sun rises moon
rises too
in the east

white
they stand long
leg'd in grass

their shadows in
star'd under
earth

this

this door I thought
went under
              (ground being
no house, or

door that was a thought
caught, creaks, houseless
in the wind on weak
hinges
          left a

jar's a limb one
live oak on
another.

"of generation"

for jeep a
scorpio

wind here
          & sun, that one
goes a long way to come
out where tides of
air are
        light like a
headliness infects

    beyond the after-rain
    webs that ring the
    picket fence

    (juniper where you
     are cocoons were

now with newfound lungs &
eyes to see by may
(as a compass word that
 lets, to encompass)

all generous tides of love & will
power you generate of sun love's
one.

'"sculptural energy is the
mountain"
          gaudier-brzeska

for satis
faction face flat blind
sun she
rubs to mine the feel of
small fur her sheer
joy

    standby/

scarcely e
nuf of touch the
sun's mechanics as the
tower did rise

          gaudy a
rodia flesh
hulled pebbles &
other small
articles of faith the
tower did rise

          tangere
noli me tangere or
snow the way she
walks off.

from VANCOUVER POEMS

Wet fur wavers

                    up a long eye-line sunday sprays
interior city ground. Aqueous cut of the sea's
a bottomless lagoon. Logs lash on. The grey
stretch of sand I walk, footsteps suckt. jumpt.

Changes air now wet as the sea, The city

        Comes walking up thru humor in the way of
vision, salt. Cedar all over. Cedar for headdress.
Beaver or bear, what is there to the touch of,
you said. Come well back into view.

                            Trappings. change.
but what runs in the middle, gestures, wired for
vision. Spirals back thru city even underground

(the long esplanades cover waves to the point
 that all of your faces echo. thru one eye. white.

Small figures as blue & white when shadows come,
Down alleyways of sight, peri winkle, vinca, small
single flower

        by the sea (Salt does, Asphalt
cuts thru time, your eye, my tongue, down where a
culvert mouths on the beach the city's underground:
You come thru walking, corpses, bits of metal,
bird cry.

'Old bird' he,

                  turned up thin his time, bones
held together by yellow & translucent parch-
meant: rags & bags & papers. His torn collar,
scarf at so craggy & knotted a neck declared
itself to be holding the trachea, thin rind of
muscle. When he opened glass to admit me a
skeleton stood, in the broom cupboard where the
toilet was. I sat. Clotted broom bristles
hugged the wall. All around, coughs & creepings
of old men trickled in under the door.

At night I heard him hack up blood, scraping it up
with his tongue (head against mine on the other
side of cardboard). Parrots in wallpaper mimickt
the sound.

              Upstairs, went to hand him the
cheque, his room a shell suckt dry & filled
with granular bird tongue. & he without his
jacket (an accident). Let loose the scarf,
sagged, into abandonment.

                    Sunday you were
still there. We sat, surrounded by glass panes
which fell out one by one from the windows. Drank
coffee, ate boiled eggs, solemnly. & all the bells
of all-day churches round about   were throwing up
their clappers.

Savary,

in short wiry sea tufts, savory, the breakers,
boat in shallows. It is sun on a length of abandoned
woodfloor. It is the sound of sand feet have worn, in
canvas shoes, in cracks of the sanded floor, in the
bottom of rattan chairs. It is the parrot a chinese
cook brought off the ships with him. It is a ship
doctor.

Glasses. clink. a man with character.

A field of lilies grown each year, fish pool, jeep, a
practice, sea wind smashing off grief point his point.
"all . of the children . run . from your arms."

This man,
old, who comes thru sun haze, a little weathered with
the difficulty of his warmth (unbending) crisis of
death a familiar, but ill-resigned hand. That grew
lilies, forced to his will flesh,   saved,   &,
cut.
will. not will (vinca, small blue flower) house now
summer   left, to rot, getting into the cushions,
somebody's embroidered shawl, rust a japannd cookie tin.
The remnants of export/exploit (opium, a dead smell of
sea poppies.)

Hero? (vinca?) None. Earth not being new.
Stray, if you must, residue
of roots, of fine savory,
Sand cover, Dawn.

Femina

                you who
                        fail,

                                subtly seeking, with your face
angled downward to the floor, to cups, to broom
slivers in the cracks, to sea below, to the
hands & feet of people walking in proximity to you.
Who wait, up in your room that sideways to the
street holds certain figures in a gloom.

When the whiteness of light casts its sheen over
your face, you sit reading. & your eyes seem closed
in their downward looking, in the electric
enumeration of eyes of strangers reading you.
& bed posts, glutted with the heads of fishing
corks, which you, as yet, can still hold onto.

All
    evening
                air slowly darkened round the windows
you were caught in, rings, on a glass jar. Coherent
images of light fisted into themselves after the
bulb had gone, just out . . . (*then* the rock cod
drift up thru blankets of the sea to reach you . . .

They flung the door open onto the city. You saw
her framed: her long. bream. skirt. ankle-tied,
heels poised on your fire-escape. The precision of
those heels. Paused, in third position, knees bent,
one fishy sleeve out, to the door . . .

                                O the fabulous
laugh of the sea trapt in a jar (o the tearing of
water.

            You are there
                        bristles of the broom are there

The bones of your face are pinned with autographs.

Morning

        makes that light up billboard face a time we
near you, clear the air we stuttered in, mid, last
night's news . . .
         Be side, by side, Beside the
water's edge we come up to, ignore bridgewise, say,
the siding of houses dark, or dank with what sea
does. There is that smell air will never get rid of.
Riddled. Or crushed by the ground coming up
                           Gravel.

We could believe in grass growing over cement in parking
lots they've turned their yards into. This billboard
fronts a house, or sides it, ferry sidling above the
abyss of bridge, Blackball Ferry, You, ferried into
'high seas' of the mind.

             This time skin has touched
thin air, raising fur (rumour). Bones razed this morning,
ear honed in the sharp gaze of a gull, bridge-poised,
momen/tarily, the rail he
stands on,
        Fence. Specific to your head a billboard
loomd above. late. in street light's desolate glare.
truck. & there you were, two of you below the sign,
swinging your legs. 'What . . . ? the cop who stopt. Only
getting some air.

         It is not instant, these houses blind to
the bay. It does not recognize a fence, this news (whose?)
rammed to the wall night has seeped into. It is constant,
rain, raising blisters,
    raising the cheap linoleum,

    Burst tomato mildewed sill

    scorch in the wood rotting
    "failure" (cockroach)

             What a rock thrown in, hit,
by design, by what casual will to break in . . .
Cupboards, cupboards, cupboards.

The Blackball Ferry
churns on thru troughs & peaks. indomitable. It is not
failure. It is not wanting. YOU want, YOU are found,
wanting, cut to the quick. By an extraordinary grassgreen the
mercury vapour lamp pours out,   for hope,   for glass

shatters love sometime.

Light. gets

        the way sun fills a, silhouettes,
pavilion (dirty) floss of worn . sandstone .
bodies make . warm.   Sudden increase wind off
water rakes.   A stare.   A cold hard measure there

wash house wall is writ: Sun.   God for a day
deadman's island made,

                       of tribe their
fireweed call it, island of the dead.   blood.
Risen as sap-engorged genitals a stare . . .

"longest days of the year this weekend mean," late,
from the Sylvia, beer sun divine, chain, some boats a
guard
           (Joe,

               the bandstand a grand
stand watch, circuitous, full path going down of
sun, moons coming on, weak (glow) popcorn stands,
their friends, dogs, small knot a cigarette makes,
fragrant joint or, incense . . .

             is an act of
living their being . WHERE . they could only be seen,
out.   "the continuing course of a life"

              His unremembered name
Joe Fortes, well appointed, self begets.   A guard.
A natural.   Quit-job, called (Seraphim of Barbados) to
sun's loom intersection of
           low light & water
                (thread

No seasonal fly of want, stays, as the popcorn sellers
warming hands (moths) to, hot butter drawn, this winter
long.

Slimey,

        mackerel seasky (eyes down). Limed,
public library steps, the. gulls. Mean what they
cry. Old men. How many step to a dead fish smell.
How would *you* like a tail in the eye, scales , a
little bit rhumey but otherwise. Off the point
they go fishing, Under latches of the bridge,
rusty, rattling their rods. Tide. Swirls down
deep there. Noon rains in the street a white lunch.

Blue hubbard figures hump, endless round the cup,
too big to get into. Does it hold anything but rain?
Steams on a hot day, the park lunches.

Hold my hand in the otherwise steamed up closet where
bread wilts. I love you but don't. throw your rain-
coat over my head. It smells. wet. hair. hangs into
my cup. Love rains. You will go far somewhere.
Where? matter inserts relation.

Peels, heels, float like hulls of hands under the
wharf. Rats dockside. Carrying orchids up, & the
port, & the starrd-on-board lights.

Milk run amalia ends up on library steps, a cigarette,
some soup. On a wet day steams up the insides of
their eyes. I want to know how gulls keep flying.

                  water, close at hand, does not close
fire. Back to an open harbour, Pier D legendary
viaduct that thousands walk
                    in time, seagulls crying,
wind, one man stone by stone laid a wall to girdle his
life round,
        canoe,
           or tombstones in a lot,
                  ties made:

VIADUCT:

        "several transcontinental trains daily" underfoot.
At foot, sea. "CPR's 14-ship coastal fleet . . . (or) regular
calls of white Empresses from the Orient"
                principally a
passenger embarcation, for, he remarked with pride, the
metropolis. Thought, high-buttoned, boots a stamp of
that civility, the Lions ranging, royalty on a cowcatcher
(snicker) view of the Rockies, O Empire. Furthest outpost
cradled inland sea the ships go down to, & they
crowded round as so many shadows view the new
arrivals

&/or necessity
        "first thing off the ship & onto the
train east . . . silk train . . . heavily insured"
              orchids,
flown in crates, "shipments" (Yokohama, Hong Kong,
Shanghai)

wait . . .

Viaduct. led West, or turning, shadows do in 'gateway
to the east' of rising sun, set, in their sunset.
London 29 days out of Yokohama! . . . "the birth of an era"
SS Abyssinia. In transit, peoples. A time of "terrific
coolie movements . . . The Chinese were going through Canada
in transit & were heavily guarded." THIS WAY. chattering
'inscrutable' antipodes to their 'frontier' . . . unseen from
the first import ('home' brought) lace, pianos, glass all
tinkly equipage

               A Parlour, refuge from the trees
CPR cleared along Water, Cordova, Hastings & Pender Streets
"by the bowling-pin method," beer parlour whisper you can hear
dice clicking nights, on Pender,
                                  wise on whatever, groggy,
with mired eyes, they view what seems most foreign:
circumambulation of cars, sight-seers, the moneyed hysteria
of night-diners, shoppers for asian curios.   Don't see.
Ducks hung, animals all sorts, coiled forms of living cured
of that dis-ease
                     he
                     stands in (Heian) old man fishing for,
off galley shithouse or pier, eyes too small a conflagration,

Alderman Bird, firechief, had "difficulty getting down the
Granville Street hill . . . because the whole road was black with
people . . . Flames were travelling underneath the dock at a
terrific pace"

A man could hardly piss so cold . . . "some one" . . . lit
cigarette perhaps.   Newspaper, even chinese, catches fast.

For what part: my city

                    monotonous under cloudblank hums,
throttle unseen, barge accidents, the fog. Merged with its
rocky margins, rain, trees' arms (internal dark) a dilute
sun records . . . scuttle of crabs in the soakt bark. The
Sudden Jerk, steaming, vacant (oolichan runs now april),
no sound towing's quite complete without . . .

    (hands, all, downed in water swell)

Not stumps of cabbage field-wise rot, in an echo of axes,
Jerry's spar, the swell. 2 men on springboards balanced pre-
carious, halfway up a trunk, hack (largest floating limb the
world . . .) crash in the undergrowth

    (snug plaid jacket, rainhat, remnant of a foot)

Even pubs this evening's closed, cross, levy their tribute for
a man none care to know. Wheels out from harbour dark.
Signals RR hotel, the Main (skid) roads annex. Spittle of
stairway yields its boards' last crack, last, gulp . . .

                      What travels west?
beside suicide, a stake in the string the junk shops pawn?

This city: shrouded (shreds) of original stands, darkened by
absence of (at the foot of Columbia Tea Swamp joined the
water's edge), its will o' the wisp, is Bukwus, old

                      drunk/ghost

                  figure of woods.

frayed paths leading, leaving . . . one-way sits,
stony, picks at, loose end of her, at loose ends,
waiting,

Beer. In beer she is sitting, sits,
Stanley, or New Fountain nights of rain. Fog warning
loud & long. A low, swish of cab, slower ("& the,
shark, bites") scythe, of cop headlights . . .

Used to see
beach far side of Water, one block down. Seeps into her
sitting, wet, in bobby sox trod. Rings the sodden
coaster on tabletop. Their edges ground by, pebbles,
fingers, all hands leave

"never, never a trace of red"

No more shattered by than one is seeing trees,
whistled at the heart of her, flesh, his does not
cut
You SPENT it!   Bitch!
Entrepreneur, white,
with indian "leman" come to beach, his British flag &
British joviality, a simple first (cash) inroad to
the maple tree's black hat & talk of 'what this town
needs,' Carrall & Water, first, to drink, to drain a
cup. They drown their whiskers in, meet, her indian
eyes . . .

Hastily, someone's idea "Maple Tree Square
would rival the public spaces of the world." Populous.
Drunks shuffle in public doorways, tired, christmas
lights, all year beer parlour fights, thin chested
bird, whistle, of their dyed hair & tongues.   The
bond still ("head," offered a swig) known by the
streets they keep, ghetto or someone, hey maggie,
knows you . . .

Go on

go on along Main, along the way, light lingers in the
goldfish bowls junk shops are made of, junk, a ship, to
sail away on, to opulent shores a commode, old needles,
her gathering flesh knows nothing of.

She strangled on the
contents of her stomach. Mostly alcohol.

Or sitting alone
along the curbs of public buildings, old Carnegie Library
closed down. Men. Pigeons. Shit all over the stone.
Thighs crossed hard, disowning their feet down steps where
they go, who can't wait to make it / to score / to go on

Agile
wits necessary as the need, How do you pull that off, the
cash, no teeth to chew on.

She died her hair
flaming red, her flesh crept inches on her as time did,
in the curved chair. Aw shit man, just gimme a bed to
sleep in, I don't care

Who writes the interoffice memos? Who built Dominion Trust?
Who reached the top of the Sun?

Some pigeons dreaming,
mordant lustre to their plumage, greens & purple, old bruise,
Blues, Fittest for what milieu?

She missed the chair,
jumping over it to reach her, fell, heavily on a wrist
(hurt? . . . get away!) & came up laughing, if cocaine
does that, I oughta try beer maybe . . .

7 hours after release
was found dead.

Who eats in this pond? At arms' length,
mostly bone. Outside, cars eat at the city's lungs, mills
eating away at the source, on the edge,

SOMEBODY's banquet
of flesh goes on.

49

        rewind, of a line (trolley tracks limp back toward,
Opens its doors to the crumbling of transfer. thin. One or
two, However late, descend. rescind. their habitual,
glare-light for (whatever reason
                straight, in the face of,
harbour's rank sewage pilings

eaten away at the foot, at the foot of so many streets,

        by a stutter of docks, wharves, jetties,
jutting where the ferry used to run, broaching the
harbour. lowdown (up to her car ramp stood staring,
at gasoline pools, peel, whatever refuse refused its
meta/
        meta.Morphosed, Under glass the coffee bar steamed,
Outside cars wet, crew in slickers & the wind, rain deafened,
fading, into wave . . .

At the door, of a steep descent,
in vinick's used furniture (mirrors, chairs), oreck's
five & ten, eskin's with its unworn fabric smell.

The body of the esplanade suffers (who walks?) Emptyness,
Of drydock, warehouse. Who, with his eyeball to the glass,
to a dummy's night waxen skin, Under the green light with
nowhere to go, thinks, in a ghostly clatter of bowling pins,
to make time (whether in fact or no), says so . . .

                Taxi,
Where the reservation, babysitters, sleeping dogs don't lie.
Down, where the end of the town's

        a street without a car
        a car without a man
        a man without a name,

              Night, ah.

But the body of the esplanade sunsets. colours of gas.
works tremendous visionary marbles crowned HOTEL. Whose
registers see only drunks. rein their collarbones in
doorways. Weathering.

Alcazar, Cecil, Belmont, New Fountain, names
stations of the way, to

Entrances

                speak doors that swing under
men's, women (& escorts, escorted by an era
gone a little later than the sawdust, smashed glass
brawls, still, the angry sweep of hand or
beer-clumsy (weighted, rolling to the floor

    (root's daughter's o
                  the waiter, watch where
you're going, threatens (snarl) big beer-belly's
MUSCLE
          means, to the door bounced exit onto
                        (desolate
light, no, POWER
          back there where friends, where
the world sits on curved chairs by little tables stackt
with glass, empty, full, empty, waiter, eight more
(weighted) take one for yourself, change
wet on the
        Changes. change is. floor caves under
& BaxbakualanuXsiwe's body "covered all over with
mouths," drops , to the pit, his red cedar bark falls.
into the hands of Hamats'a

                    a drumming & a singing
pulse. rock charged air smokes (the red smoke of
his house? smokes Mountains, "at the mouth of"
river-running sea

        Whose heart heavy with ferocious lips,
to see, legs, hips, tits, to want? the taste of flesh.
or whose small hair.
        With a violent gesture wipes out the
bar, the primitive order of barkeep, bouncer, copcar, court
or,
    construction

(*use the men's entrance*) is the construction
we put upon it, his glass, his chair someone takes or someone's
eye upon his wife. *Men's, women's.* & the separate washroom
doors they vanish into. The private law. He said I put the
finger on him, pickt up outside, fingered, it is all alien,
property, Is what belongs to another, Her tight dress no
trespassing but still, come in —

                         We live by (at the mouth of)
the world, & the ritual. Draws strength. Is not Secret
a woman gives (in taking, Q'ominoqas) rich within the
lockt-up street. Whose heart beats here, taking it
all in,
       Nanwaqawe: Who are you?
       She: Your daughter (didn't you know?) Initiator.

Who is rooted to the floor with a root so deep he cannot
shovel it. Singing:

"The hamats'a mask of the forehead, the hamats'a
  mask of the whole world, the prettymask . . ." &

"The red cedar bark of the whole world is making you
  voracious"

       . . .

            O little man, o little man with dull eyes,
with 3 full glasses at closing time, I take you in.

Air

a blanket, a wind, the sea flooding in, to harbour

sand flat. off the north shore. spit, with harbour mark,
not buoy, small white lighthouse shape, the light, thunder
of cars on the bridge above

                       & the lights ahead

at reservation's edge, weed soft, flash of sea on aura of
light, in the water ahead

blanket, a wind, the sea flooding in, to harbour, wind,
off the deck of ferry rounding a black flank of park,
for the chain arc the bridge is (lit / causeway to, into.
ENTER

           arena of dark (at this hour empty) LIGHT:

car will rattle into off a wooden ramp man points the
way from, lockt blocks, dull-lit bus standing on its round . . .
ferry now behind us, passenger-hollow, & the engines idle,
all its lights on, all its cars dispersed . . .

                                What is this
space between bodies of land a canoe rides, putting out from
the shelter of a bay. This. drowned. coast. the Salish
(Squamish at, tidal flat under the bridge) sea-going, saline.

Embraced a pool of contact . . .

                    Islands with common feet under
the waves the air
                waves
                    on our skin. we stand in. rooted.
outside car wind swept dark, incoming tide, silent other cars.
Silent? We are. In the wind coming into harbour, sea a
tidal race, & blowing, into our mouths, into (moving now)
our mouths'. full. kiss.

                shoes sink in.   mulch.   toes curl (away from,
crumbles in the hand some (late) stump heart.   Only
casing what was, is, riddled with the weather, riddle of
achieved height now
                          desuetude or, crumbs left,
pieces of flesh dangling (shreds) the wood ticks or worms
eat thru
           to
                    air, acrid & earthen.   Water brackish, fern
the dead wood's only.
                     green

                         Each moment (monument)
at the edge of each, Pioner Mill then Moodyville,
inlet, & from Hastings Mill, small fires curling,
saw whine at water's edge the chips. fly where they
will.   But not. not "Moody's men   went dry &
worked sober."   For each, inlet adrift with it,
Smoke . . .
                 a sea   Bear comes down to thru mountain
ravine, eyes watering, small eyes, red, windows Set,
the sun, catches early —

                  be changed, grow fur (as logs at sea do)
be, Bear Mother screwed by a bear's by a giant

                    (will, make Moodyville, the dryest
                     settlement the inlet's. financial.
                     success

                     who died at sea)

What we called "fort": its bark exterior still stands,
jagged & high enough to crouch within, fingering
what scrapes under nail or, palmlines silted with it,
waiting, for what?
                     (face down in the
                      dirt in the
                      grass of broken
                      glass

Young wood carved & painted, will, stand tall mid
dark the branches weave now, locus abandoned as a
burnt out house
                        to represent, flaunt (taunt) the
would-be EVENT, whistling in the deep wood

"As it is, they lean precariously, tottering in every
wind . . . destined to crash down, one by one," while

sometimes, finally, trees grow up around them.

from RINGS

Rings, iii

And the bath is a river, in the quiet, i bring only candle
light, in the corner by the faucet, shadows leaping, steam.
& the window. Outside a fresh wind is frothing the apple tree,
its own river streaming, round the house,

          like a dream,
There is no story only the telling with no end in view or,
born headfirst, you start at the beginning & work backwards.

It was a dream, a report in the newspaper Norman was reading
(it was reported of him telling) he was born in the small
house/shack at the back of 443 Windsor (the street where
we lived—it must have been in the 100's) a big old tree,
dust, & the dilapidation of the main house where they later
lived, all this against a very blue sky that belonged to the
girl the paper said had come out to the coast for health reasons
& stayed, fell in love with the mountains & sea & made frequent
trips by ferry to the island

      (& Al was on the phone i was
saying but feel the ribs of the baby you can feel them in me
(ribs? his or mine?   contractions of muscle, something muscly
& unborn

    that she had in some way redeemed him, he painted
for her or whatever he did that was to make the paper report
his beginning.

    & when i woke up i remembered that Norman had
drowned in a river in the interior in his teens. But not before
i'd thought the past is still alive & grows itself so easily
i must set it down, pre-dawn of a sunny day, Wet, birds in the
half dark singing, trees only just beginning to unfold their
leaves . . .

    the sea, ferry she was on, small, crossing it, the
sea he looked down on, was the ease of his telling it, where
he is.

In the bath a sea my belly floats in, i float
relieved of his weight——he floats within.   & the genetic
stream winds backward in him, unknown, son of a father once
fathered.

Tell him, in the bath in the quiet (wind & the bell
clanging outside) only this restless streaming night, fresh
wind off the sea, is where he is.   Water, candle changing in
the draft, turns slowly coool.   Ripples when i lift my fingers
edge around this streaming, in the river-sea outside that winds
around our time, this city, his father's father . . .

'delivered'
is a coming into THIS stream.   You start at the beginning
& it keeps on beginning.

Rings, v

Time to go in, from the afternoon grass, lifting him,
nudging the pram under shadow of the house.   From after noon
sun keeps pouring, light we live in, thick with, smell of
grass fresh cut down the street, bird song, hour after hour
the cats, wary in long grass hunting elusive wings.   His face
hardly tanned, eyes hurt in light, careful, turning with him
in my arms to keep his face dark

turning, wheeling with him in
my arms, hand up shadowing his eyes, from light, intensive sky
blue, into blue under, shell light over the radii of trees
reaching their upturned arms high overhead, my head, over
his, the cats' eyes filled, all, luminous cavity of brain,
with light:

this newborn (reborn) sensing, child i am with him,
with sight, all my senses clear for the first time, since
i can remember, childlike spinning, dizzy . . .

'What go—es up, must co—me down.'   Up the back steps, stagger,
hold him up lightly for my arms to absorb the shock to him
(springs) as once my water did.   & into, shoulder against
the door, dark kitchen smell people have lived in, years
(old lady, all her windows nailed against the sun).   Now,
door ajar for cats, it lightens, wind blows thru our curtains,
sun pours into the front room i see it, crossing the back,
shine along a length of wooden hall.   His room's still faint
blue under the white, red curtains made so air moves specks of
colour, yellow, breathe.

And laying him down (my arms unroll, un-
burden) on the white sheet, he begins to kick, anticipating
diaper change, yes, wet.   Unpinned now, folded on the can lid,
heat will condense in little drops by the time i get back &,
now his legs are waving free, he likes that, smiles, fists
waving too, slow motion underwater dance is both, reeds, & the
dark at the back of my eyes . . .

imminent dizziness from heat. from
light to dark.   too dark.   Concentrate: red buttocks: cream
(cold & white). big balls & penis & the fabric soft against them.
Folding in to pin, he doesn't like that, cries.   Have i poked him?
No. Ever?   Maybe natural fear of binding, or my apprehensive
fingers.   Hi blue eyes, funny face so blue

as the sea, unknown.
what you see, when will you smile TO me? (believing already you
know who, in the hospital gaze at my hair, my mouth, & know my

voice.) But smile? They say it's gas fleeting, pucker. whimsy.
You know, little one. with smallest frown unfocused between
your brows. Hungry? Yes, it's time.

                                    & light. Wind's blowing
the curtain, see, patterns of light like waves falling
across the floor. & cool now on my skin, unbuttoning
blouse, evaporates, my sweat from the sun gone. You?
cold? The cotton blanket, all your things, that delicate
smell you're wrapt in, new. But you must smell the
grass on me, sweat, insects, earth? These things you'll
spend hours with. All right, i'm hurrying. & the milk's
already dripping. That's your world. Hunger surge, mouth
open already crying. pain? There, into the rocking chair's
familiar fabric against my back, elbow up to support your
head, & nipple lifted towards. You're drinking now, those
hungry sucking movements of mouth, palate like little fish.
And snuggling down myself into the chairback can relax now,
So, The day is still,
               Again,
                      This world. Something precious,
something out of the course of time marked off by clocks.
Wind blows, plants breathe out their odours drawn by sun,
drifts, gradually over the house, shadows the back lane
lengthen, birds too, active at different times remark,
their wings worms' activity, the day's age . . . daze, an
age was all i knew, child in blue sea dress & bare legs,
climbing from terrace to terrace. Uncalled (from home),
called, by the focus of an orchid, length of tree shadow,
sun a glint on sea below, the island light, passing from
mainland out, to sea, to see *where* time turns, known by
intensity of odours, orchids', & the earth here,

                                  Here's

lilacs outside your window. Lilac time i brought you home in.
Thick fragrance up the back lane our car drove thru, Al
drove thru, ecstasy, to be outdoors again, get out on grass,
springy, unlike cement or hospital floors my feet had known
a week, & you had never known it, smelt, the sun. in every
blade, leaf, culm. breathing light. & never known the
lilacs i'd thought of old lady flowers a dying, virulent as
fever (ecstasy

               Cold at my heart ('must co—o—me down'),
times you're so quiet (sleeping) when i bend can't tell if
you're breathing still. & Al: of course he is. The cats,

Conch in your crib the other day. by suffocation. sudden
death. Wake up suddenly past the hour you should have woken
cried for milk, Come running down the hall, fear at my throat,
The time, the time it takes to reach your door, open it,
draw near (slow motion, slow, reluctant) Find you sleeping
still.
    The fear.
               Stops. Up my heart, stops breath. Stop
The circle ('spinning thru,' 'Drop, all your troubles by the
river, side, Catch a painted pony on the spinning wheel ride.')
Which does spin on thru. It's fear of the unexpected, of
the music suddenly broken off. It's fear of it happening
When . . . ? ('Is the music over, Mom?')

            'Let the spinning wheel spin.'

                           & the pressure
built up til it hurts in the other breast, is full, towel
tucked under wet, & you, long hard pulls now, almost empty,
time to shift you. Lift you up, little head on my shoulder,
stroke that burp that never comes between times, only after,
only they say, burp him between breasts, & I grow tired of
hurting, & you, maybe want some more, or maybe fall asleep,
already? I put you down in my arm, left side i never can
arrange it right, so your nose is free to breathe & your
head not turned in some way awkward as the other never is.
Left side, sinistra. But you're eager. No need to suck,
it's there, drip from the nipple, tho you do, must, i figure,
your gulping that swift, spurt, like a water fountain down
your throat.
          Connect. Open conduit, light or liquid flowing
thru. you. in the circle my arms make around you drinking
sun, my own, skin, hair absorbed, what you now take in. all
that you need.
            Tho it seemed so thin looking when it first
came, in a milky water. all the nutrients are there. &
still it runs. more as you want more, grow more. Amazed,
at the interconnection still. Those first days how, with
every suck, i could feel the walls of uterus contract. You,
isolate now, & born, healing my body for me.

No wonder he grows strange, feeling so, outside. Never comes
in when he comes home, only sometimes, news to tell. But
usually (no news? bad news) heads into the kitchen or the
bathroom. Ritual of coming home. Jacket on chair (hot?)
sleeves rolled up, neck open (tired & edgy) heads for ice,

scotch. The end of a cement day of hospital floors. Walls.
Still there.

Walls & clocks he has to move by. Watch (face
of the sun) he never takes off, wound by the action of his
wrist each day a myriad gestures, tasks, the way he writes,
backhanded. Backwards (stubborn), moving back.

Last night's
dream sat up in the middle of the bed to hold him, catch him
falling thru a confusion of falling Kit was him. & only
woke him.

Fear.

Stopt the wheel, the music falling out of
time. & 'the painted pony,' Rides on up & down, riderless.
retreating.

The unborn.

Who-is-it? lives, a dark unknown.
No two feet on the ground, no gravity in water, no sense of
weight. His own, his own weight known to him.

My fear's then
not that you die who i've barely known, but not be born. Not
bear yourself alone & learning it, your birth into the light of
day, dazed, the risk we all take, pushed out into it.
No one a mother to you, no—the uterus itself contracts
& pushes its burden out. At a certain point (in time)
ripe as a fruit, a weight, the intimate night's expelled.
made light. made isolate one in the world,

the wheel. My
arms make around you spinning as the world does, we wheel thru
light & dark. One day's going (birds & wind, leaves tightening
as our warmth does) into night.

What can i tell you,
little one, that you don't already know? Nestled there
half asleep, yet sucking, dreamy, open to milk, to all you
want & all that afflicts you, hunger, gas, light, irritation.
Self contained there in my arms that weigh the burden of you.
Your small face. Knowing, Unknowing, I will bend over,
shade you plantlike as the sun turns, deepening toward
suppertime & the night, light outside your window cut
off by the house, by five o'clock.

Cars whirr by outside, gravel spews. (A certain motor.
Gears down, stops. News from outside coming home.

from COLUMBUS POEMS

Columbus will

turtle neck strain
eyes cry see
for dream's sake

    (remarks, a
       moony head

somebody up there
doesn't like me, late
face again

        (how
          human to be
          hands out
          wanting smiles

around the deck

no Noah's flop of
comedy's respect

    (a hope
    a 'seen' a

        moon—

hands feet do kick out
(anger at

small turtle hates
being overturned

turtle for name
"Tommy" we gave
sight, sound, smell etc
how we know, or you

                    WHO
                "can you
                hear me?"

    Cid, the split
    knowing & feeling
      "doesn't know he
    only wants to sleep"
    doubts
              you cry for the
              world at times over
              much

              want

    no ears to hear
    my tiptoe, wake
    at the smallest
    who-comes, clair
    audient
              Taurus

                        mix-up of
                        animal i
                        dentity, these
                        creatures we
                            live with
                        mobile of
                        moo
                              graar
                                    the blue
                        hooves or shell crystalline

    tortoise before the
    new world brought
    turtle up
              a long
                        trip to
    reiterate

              the unseen
              things we live with
                  (Indies possibly

                    63

to
sleep, turtle, dream
your patchwork shell of
memories at 6 months you
anticipate
          (imminent
          'boo' yet

          the sea creeps up unknown

see, you
sleep

sky lullaby

"3
men in a tub"
come
stopping his cry

     windy
           odour of
           up from
           no teeth to
           brush, gum
           semi
           transparent

exotica just this
unknown

           sun, dull, lit
           grass
           summer's end
           shone
                momen
                tarily con
                trary to
                environs

                        come

singing or crying
3 men do
in light of gum arabic or gum
of some instinctive
westerly
           passage, Pizarro
           blood run sea
           swell engirdle

           Cortez, a short
           livd man

Columbus
in deference to
environs hung
the pull of re
lationship
           to moon
                    (now trash

"fishing for" I sung him
"stars," the 3
mythopoeiac
travellers of
sky a sea we

      live in
      nor can escape

parkt
by cedar
boughs the wind
   (to)
his crying un
seen
      ripple
            Chris
            topher Magellan o
            cean I
            swung you in

look out

I worry
cold, does he
crowing, half
distress, half
exercise

Columbus
on the lookout see

    birds wheeling
    wing meaning

new way to
solace
      /one

finger to
the wind

for Kit, your

chuckle, it
breaks at
larynx, a
bubble
     ticklish
     response upon

       (leaf rustle

you chuckle
like some windy tree
air current
breaks up thru

you 'break up'
seeping whole into
'the world'

       out where the inner
       man begins
       on edge

       a laugh
       sometimes provoked

irritable
leaf mimosa curling
water
     salts your
       laughter
       close to tears
         streaming

downstream leaf floats
minute boat calling
at the bank where current
holds some respite

       we say dallying

       the world of
       stream, rock, reed

wind blows, boat
calls
into & out of
small boy world
we do not know

what you find funny, near
hysteria, the tree
that thru you streams
        its face calling
now you see me, see

        how does it look
        to you? the trees

rustle, sing, & not
wind which
rustles leaves
its trace only
evident as ash
of fire?

        "The ash
          is the tree of sea-
          power . . . of power
          resident in water"

                                    strangling other roots
                                    little Woden, Wotan

rides thru time beats
thru the future
                bearing
in your root will ancient
tree of the world

against its end

                Woden ride
                the Night
                mare
                        Columbus astride
                unknown sea to
                the edge

this point ticklish
this bubbling hysteric
  source
       this well-
being

wind blows, wind
calls
   one
particular leaf, you

run downstream to meet
my leaf, life

  we also

  touch

from WHAT MATTERS

let

yr cock mine
a dark
light ahead

seek that
collapse of wall we
sometimes give in

will
what doorway's spent

    that lock

emptiness wears
lockt tight in it
self lockt

        hands
        will work

whose invention is
a door again

unlockt, opens on
some shared dark
carbide / car
nified

    Light—

what the cock knows
beyond crowing, spent

Of orange trees (angelica?) see green: as what the eye needs
morning when oil glazes skin. heat. (of the day's not to be
yet) this freshness, freshet, water, lifting the glass to lips,
comes on a sweet taste

                        after sour? Night. Night's mouth
sour—grapes at not being able to . . . Repeat: they had got up
first, & bright. Our entrance from the hall must (from the
dark) have struck them as blind, day begun some hours already.
We see them small with table between, engaged in some kind of
close . . . 'out on the verandah' . . . morning: hits the face.
Or did he see them close? or even notice. Our choosing of
seats conservative (stumble): each woman between 2 men or
the reverse. Corners. Each to his own, her place.

                                  Faces white
with day raise distance (blank wall ahead, is the form of a
question): A turning towards me (not) could watch trees past
D's head to building's edge; C opposite has that surge in full
view; D also turning to . . . a green eye juggles with

                               HEAT, skin
exposed his glance made no comment on: heat's small sweat
beads over forehead, upper lip. Of orange angelica (preserve
some sweetness) see green water we last swam in, A & me, in
silence, shine. 2 women below with kids undress, voices rise
(splash) nonsensical (what to do, do, not how) their children
calling, see me see me . . .

                       to preserve (angelica) the moment
of falling. All children wish to see themselves, to be seen . . .

as 'up some hours already' (what have YOU done with your dawn?)
can be clarity at this hour, here only white, siding behind C's
head (or tipsy leaning?) 4 geometric on 4 legs rickety each on
flooring (at the mouth of a minehead

                         on pickaxes, they stand
some a little drunk their grins or tipsy leaning, lean over,
falling . . . she. was stung by insult or. bore him heavily to
the point. in the photograph small, stands solemnly contained,
one man's arm slung easily round her neck, restraining . . .

Yesterday dusty as what lies in the town museum after (night's excitement). Little boots. Even axes look small. Or a revolver fits in the palm almost miniature.

Surely it's the aftertaste gone sour that wakes us.

So, 'climbed the hill looking for coffee. no place open' even (sounds of the street: a bell) dog only solitary (tolls, heat takes its toll) a morning kitchen help might sleep. angelus. Some inevitable pacing of the day here (their plates of ham look good)

slam: screen door air wisp hair, tired face, or tired of sundays' sameness: ham coffee juice eggs.

had said 'any chance of coffee?' oh past her he recognized someplace her leisurely walk. Banters, redhead? No, the one with the tight ass . . . scene from somewhere: that quiet glimpse of someone's kitchen, still-hung pots depend, her flesh, its working. Hadn't even noticed. Does A?

She says even before that (evening, she had gone to bed first, 3 of us sitting in chairs under the orange tree, 2 of us close) sun woke him, or anyway never sleeps in, read , every page of the sunday paper. Needs patent (walls between) all that activity light thru newsprint . . .

only woman hanged, it said, in this part of the country. no angel yet . . . she had her reasons.

Look, mama, look. Mama! (breakfast comes. her hand. blue plates of ham grease won't jell on.) Look at me. I'm looking. No, LOOK at me. (coffee cuts. the stawberry taste of jam good with ham.)

D now on his 4th or 5th cup, wiping drops from moustache, hears what (eyes down) she comments: thinks the whole town should wake when he does (all that silence out there), don't you, love? Unanswered. Mouth makes its gesture rue some bitter pip (oldtime. old town. this town a movie set we sit in, picturing ourselves.

73

I'd said, Yellow—the after
noon haze enthusiasm plays, for the image, A, will you take a
picture of the street? (climb thru window to verandah's edge)?
in view of the drop, grange or masonic hall's impossible stone
furthering windows, way in . . . He said take it from the street.

As from the street, WHEN're you coming to bed?

So need infects
the dream breath swells (unripe oranges last night slit by his
knife, green, hardly sections, or sectioned like some minute
flower pattern, unflesht as yet)
'The stink of your mouth at
breakfast'. . . a deep slap?   If it hurts she only smiles.

Coffee
increases sweat, or secretes violence.   Her hand level as any
man's to shoot him down.

Saloon set last night in theatrical
light of window piece, by piece, 1895, no not a date he said—
a number men remember.   O the tiffany there you would not believe,
liqueurs, preserved sweets, swell tits their fingers unruffle,
largesse or, pianissimo!   to raise us.   They laugh together . . .

One.   shot in the dark.   Will she see us when she comes down?
Double shot mid rows of bottles oh her small face appear, collar
up, out to sea, gravity of unmoved clang of the bar (boys)
nightlight . . .

A's voice makes furred toward her.   presence
at the table cuts.   Not pathos, pathetica, heart-shape face.
Something dates her . . . angelique?   as of liqueur that was popular
then, speaking of men, midway between the angels &.   it is that
slight tension walk she does, a line to maintain herself against
any falling for.

Or jumping-off place: they are into machines
that play violin & piano combined.   they are into bottles &
gaslight & little boots . . . I said how old do you think that
trunk is?   which sits a yard or so behind me in this bar in
which . . .

A's voice light with the last 5 minutes, the 'last' double, the 'last' cut in a medley that lights & colours his passing, coins changed, whirr of memory searches for, toward, continues on past . . .

I get up alone—was the trunk inviting hands, eyes? Whose lid lifts heavy & round to imitate a chest (bust) must of paper space to lie in, hide in, pack it all in—like them, no date anonymous. D: a good idea. means, you've stepped outside the set. stopped.

Walls to remember, walls to project desire, not even newsprint casts some light on—an abandoned piece of luggage. abandoned wants, set in the museum after. She at least, she acted on them.

Drain the last bit of orange from the glass: tipt up, throat exposed to morning throbs, continuous life-line of want. & tho the verandah slopes we sit on, into that space heat poses . . . orange tree vertical, its relief of green . . .

Will that be all now? (last drop) Who so stands, pencil poised, waiting for the smallest nod to add us up, slap by A's plate ('thank you' upside down), no smile even, to collect the plates.

Unripe oranges & a morning walk. What I know of him. Was last night only audible scene. Hurried steps outside shutters 2 feet away. Heels. click click. angry. click. or hurried (don't know what to think) . . . Oh come on. (Firmer footsteps after) Don't you touch me. Let's go / Let go! (off the deep end) & his 'wait' urgent now: was she going to jump?

Silence prior to, as silence maintained in the museum after, space for wants to contract in. So we move into the must of hall in single file mount the stairs. Windows open, shutters open, cool from the as yet unsunned street. unphotographed. & this was ours.

To A: you missed the balcony scene. What? Coming to bed so late (a bad shot). What scene? She didn't jump or shoot. in anger. as I could see (so late, so isolate): You hide from me & I'll hide from you. Wide of the mark. (Was it a wrong move? for arms, his, to surround.)

75

Back in the car, luggage stowed, up out of the dead end street,
into highway sun streams in the pines high up, hair tied . . . D
with his arm around C, eyes what streams by in the splash of
window frame says: Good idea that firewood in the trunk—did
you see it?   See?   The whole set, false front, the frame,
go up in flames.

Delta

faces the
surface of
water

make rain seas
in the world maintain
equilibrium equals

balance, comment, rushing
mountain streams or plain
ditches on the
dyke road

skinny & feminine under
rain hats hide
(rushes, rushing odour of
  cabbage
            eyes only
hands pluck cut
center from floral
decay

      its smell of
flower stem left
forever in
fetid vase,

      you said our
car never
gets
stuck

o miz estrus

who rides composed, immigrant to this city,
longtime resident.   in shadow, shallow   (who knows?
nothing of tides.

o miz estrus who rides, whose mouth is
the mouth of rockcod, rocked, open & shut down avenues of
sun, bus on big tires braking

who rests, who swallows (air)
light, mouth, of onions & goodday uttered late absorbed
in fading, deeper than rust in photograph . . .

whose nights leak out in brush raccoons reveal each raid
their brief history of blood . . .

whose pads &
tailored blouse & nether panties soak in the heat of
bus upholstery, sun going down, going home,   counts
on revolutions of meter, amount of water,   whose gold
sleeps under her bed in a chinese coffer . . .

& stores the moon
(against what catastrophe?

o miz wellwrapt
shadow of a shadow, mum,   the sun . . . infuses window
(honey) widening, opened on clover stir, a breeze, a
tide of grasses barefoot o

your hands mutter & dart,
rockcod in the shadow of your thighs, while faces outside
unseen, matted, lions roar

in revolution, revels of the
SUN . . .

largely sea

at, eye
cloud your
silence casts

   a light

spray   sea
islands us
out of the waves'
crash we stand

        stranded

        pebbles stript
        of liquid
        r's l's roar

        how one word cast

light, define
in midst of a
(mist a
deafening
sound

        this man
        bows out

            taub, deaf
              or stupid
            dau-, dead
            daubs unreceptive to
            impressions, blind

in a fume i'm left
to smoke
your absence out

beyond rocks can't
make mental categories
stick
        (your agates don't
        count

79

*ig*land, *ēa*
land, not water, eye
frays us just
so far see
what can't be
made out

       frei, free

belonging to
one's own
daufr
    tho that be

listen, just one
   pebble
pickt up, suckt
cuts both ways:

      no savour without taste
      no salt but sweat, yours
        or mine to make

      a little noise.

Getting there

Carp, carp on, tooth . . . biting at rain. Almost to an ache,
city-way the salmon, gliding, never feel it on their
surface, Make it thanks to rivers.

       Linked hands or gills,
Gulp at the air where air caresses our strange backs, bellies
submerged successful, system the fish move in,

         As that day
winter moved into the lake, fingers, selves all bracken
where they used to slink, hooks deserted now. Mysterious
fish swim further downlake, deeper . . .

       Carp stays. Always
that tooth aggressive into the air, just piercing gum . . .

Carp on they say, talkative, females of the race, a genius
characterized by, rise to the occasion, Words, vacuous as
kites. Race the air currents tug at strings for opening
mouths, gulp, air tails are laid in. As i'm jealous of her,
she-fish, her ease. Myself divest of aches, pain, Rain's

a festival the way it gentles us now, We bend in to see
the sky's immense racks of rainwear,

       Naked our skins swim
this element, those kites, paper, shouting the wet air . . .

Persephone to Hades

for Warren

given to clear
water & the calm after
heart's constriction

      croci still poke
      yellow white
      stands out over
      dark the
      child makes

his entrance other
strange
      groundfarer
heel-caught
mid center's core
cordialis
      /heart

thought:

your access on emotion
hard to bear, bare
heart schemes

        Persephone
        i think you know

to whom
apparitions come
homeward, struck
    dumb
opening up

under my feet
talking to you
wind sound
3 crows' flight

  not final, no
unearthly cavern holds
Persephone under

we share
thin air
difficult to breathe
at times, after all
surrounding
flesh streams
meet to dwell in

i'll tell him
air is where we
live, cliff
wise
      crocus
of accidental upper
reaches of the
atmosphere

i'll tell him, bulb
& bird

pushing light's a
delicate balance will
assert itself

despite the pull of old
worlds

"mostly sand"

does VIADUCT
Georgia Street our past
bridge to Main make

      a bond?

transcend our coming in &
going, daily
             ties cut?

i'm all bridge
today, even rail
road we somehow
more than leaving indicates
both love

         torn down in
         memory a
         sequence of
         dead nights

severed
since going, shaky, is
speedup only
15 miles i said
it will collapse, but you
they made them solid in
those days

viaduct or way
across
      leading maybe
to a concourse we believe
extant, via this
decrepit

        bridge

ardour's

fire light
livd in from
within

    wind
blowing around this
fire, does not burn
higher

        heart light's so
        withdrawn

        we do not warm
        our hollow
        backt upstate
        snow's ground we
        walk on

                walkt on past
                your eyes you
                from outside—

outside
fields tonight contract
tomorrow's quarrel
never without its
shadow under
empty moon

call, turn, come back

who'd suspect we'd endure
cold night below zero tracks
to our front, jays at the back

        bits of meat, of
        scrap, love is the
        moonlight only

                breath smoking
                dream out

release this flesh, this
stript meat even
some bird uses, meagre, to
refuel its spin-off
returning

                    empty, down

a moonlight, snow make
heartfire impossible, im/
possible from

                        outside to in
                        dream enter

ember

we see what might be
us in there, our
ardour dying ash
    poor ash & us

the poorer

first cause

this morning sun i saw rise
silent over the empty house
my love two lives now
cheerios in hand, smiles

     beatific

        morning

            son

not mythic, just
begotten one

coming home

if it's to
get lost, lose
way as a wave
breaks
     'goodbye'

i am not speaking of
a path, the 'right'
road, no such
wonderlust

weigh all steps
shift weight
to left or right to

a place where one
steps thru all erratic
wanderings down to
touch:

i am here, feel
my weight on the wet
ground

Broke   5/72

What did who pick up & throw away? both, or either? Was it
the grass grown sweet to chew in may, in let me, maybe, tell
how sea enrapt us, audience to its sound we sat, caught,
on a single chord,

& that was when we were almost simple, simply almost children,
or barely out of it, our simplicity we kept, a long time.

A child breaks children, or, broken up, we fall into the scattering
fragments of our day, a world he wanders in, as I, now he, picks
dandelions for me to sniff. I have a yellow nose on his 4th
birthday, & the sea is only (lonely) where the freighters come,
to remind me occasionally of sawdust barge & sun, glinting,
flat on the water as I raced to meet him then. Now he, is 3,
& walks steadily, picks flowers, rides trains, calls names . . .

There were always spaces of water between us & now there have
been land spaces where the moon has not landed, turned to dust,
without air or place to grow we grew lifeless, as the moon equals
the space between us our story did not run into, but on, under
water where the telephone cable lies, cut, or the car runs off
the cliff racing to meet the ferry & time, in fact, does not
exist. The story does? There is a space of green grass &
dandelions. One here one there one to pick, the sun, comes up.
Does it? Does he see lion when he says "the raahr" is
coming to get me, Sweet, smell of tobacco in old pants pocket.
old wrapper, green, of sail. stale smell his kiss aureoled by
sun suddenly, name, son, mane . . . There is never anything else?
Untrue.

Rocks break. Grass greens. & rain drops eternally on the
power line.

        If at any point this story doesn't break in two
but runs, on . . . there is only the unfamiliarity of the world to
thank. That one can, that she is, walking, continuously . . .
that streets do continue, in whatever unmapt instantaneous
projection. foot by foot. that one can, that she is, walking
without direction along a street in the west end past the
Veterans' Affairs, unfamiliar, down an alleyway of windows

to the bay. That a man suddenly intercepts her path,
cutting from a cross street, & walks ahead to a shadowy
building whose balconies covered with wire mesh (children
falling? drunks? or pigeons?) drags his leg, whose jeans
are lopsided at the hip, who disappears. That it's 10
o'clock & the Unemployment Commission has been open 2 hours.
She put her claim in the box & walked out, into the sun &
rain. When she gets in & drives, the car which is 16 years
old, keeps stalling, & people with missions to run, lean on
their wheel & honk at her.

          In Pigeon Square, some who are
nowhere, no one, sleeping already there on stone benches,
refuse, from the outdoor workers' strike, refused, like
copcar blue sharks swinging by unlit, to move. The light
falls evenly from the sky. Are we underwater? in the mounting
nausea of the morning, hotel doors swing open, noisily, open
& shut. Brilliant, sweater grown full in the wind from the
harbour hardly (concrete, how to believe in freshness when a
geranium pales, with milk, on a northern sill), she is talking
loudly with her friend. I'm looking at everybody's shoes.
You creep, didn't anyone ever tell you? Pay'n Save, on meats,
cheese. Pay, pay. How tantalizing, (thirst is, or the belly-
ache, around noon) almost across from Pigeon Square, it isn't
fair. If you lie down on your stomach on warm cement, does it
go away?

          A great big gob of spit. & the ends of her toes are
walking on it down the street in front of her sandals. He is
used to it. Catarrh at the back of his throat mixd with blood
(tar, they're tearing up the street to get at the water mains,
so strange, what's there underfoot. I mean candy wrappers,
tobacco, transfers . . . across, great distances for blocks & blocks,
cement walks up & down walls feet slip inside of, eyes cohabit,
leather, ain't so fuckin much, just, to get your hands on . . .

I love you, creep. Go home.

          (Where on earth?

To the heart of the matter: no place to root but in the heart
(stumbly, even so she holds the door open for him) so impoverished,
the retinue of those alone only rub shoulders in the alcohol/cazar
(your number? your number's up. follow the white line & walk
downstairs with care / c.a.r.s. / stare

What the fuck *you*
lookin at? never seen a man die? slowly.

He's shaking, inside the
Army & Navy doors, bargain annex. Can't tell how much he sees.
His buddy's got his hand on his arm. She has the air of cynicism her
hooked nose, pickd skin has brought on, long eyes of looking at
goods, no wherewithall. Joe, this is Shell. She'll help ya. She's
a good gal. She'll help ya buy a shirt, Joe.

Does the message get across? If I'd loved you any better would it?

The lines begin at home, at centre, where the telephone wires
come in from outside, where the rooms *they* lived in were other
worlds like the globe on her bedroom window against a rock wall,
she wanted to know what that was like, out at sea, she wanted the
weather of, always whether it was, anything other than herself,
Cordova & Hastings, don't get out of the car, where the ferry
docked, past St. James looming, monstrous above the coroner's dark
office, grocery, groceries, l.c.b., what does he want? Don't
talk to him. What did *she* want?

Since we do half the dying, we
ought to do half the living, some woman said. Oh god. It wasn't
money. But the walls, the walls. What if every suburban woman
did time on Pigeon Square?

The door shuts. The window is
rolled up. If power has anything to do with it . . . that kind of
power. It's a closed system. They live in closed-off rooms. *We*
do,

walking over the cliffs on a sunny afternoon, past the summer
house perched on rocks above the sound, watching the tugs go by,
down a drop of some 200 feet the water swirled, licking the foot of
what we stood on, swallowing boom scraps & seaweed, licking its
chops at us 200 feet behind the railing over lateral rocks hot in
the sun & tempting to stretch out on. He wouldn't let her hold his
hand who was almost 3, stumbling in hurry to follow us, wait for me,
but hauled him up on his hip & carried him all the way round the
point. Echoes: where is the house? where is the house with tarpaper
roof that runs in the sun? & the fishboats up on dock, old timbersmell,
& ropes/ me in to the past, which wells up like sea here, years
becalmed in what the future held with him who is now absent I said,
knowing nothing of children except ourselves, if you die, meaning,
if you leave, as you did, I hope I have a child by you.

That something,
something is retained. A false impression. Grass springs up each year.

Later he was angry & said, what am I? just some babysitter?
you leave me to do all the work. But you wouldn't let him hold
my hand, you do things & then say you feel used, why don't you
stop doing them?

Which opens up the crack in the world.
Why don't you, why don't you stop doing them? Cracks in the
sidewalk all my dreams have fallen into. Holes. In my shoes,
or in my seeing, so

I stop, & the world stops, & the grass.

No stopping here, he says, this street continues
down the cement blocks & the lights. Down there, where you step
into a hall, lamps are low & they are all, elsewhere, except the woman
in red who swears / little lady he says, cool it, & she laughs, she
swears they are all dead down there, c'mon what's with you guys?
The man with the cane does not look at her, the other, half-hearted,
has given up. She is gay, she is mad. Nobody here knows how to
dance. you bastards. nobody knows. Fingers grip the glass around its
waist & lift to lips, to face, this liquid foamy splash & trickle,
weak, down one side of the tabletop, this towel blots everything up.
No fucking around here. & when she staggers into the light, a
blur of colour past the guitarist who sings to the rest,
& when she staggers into the dark, it goes, this street—
or is there, out there, at the slam of the door, another world
beginning?

just inside the door. Or out. It's fog, late
morning cloud damp. No, this morning, just got up, foggy head,
pulled the plastic curtains in the bathroom, & stared up between
two houses: a bleary sun trying somehow to shine thru the level
layer of cloud, or fog today, off the warm sea Sunday beach, the
man said, I've lived here all my life, I know when autumn's
coming, you can smell the cooler air. But august isn't half
over! I said, it can't be.

Morning sleep-in & fall creeps up.
Went down thru a house filled with coffee. Sheila's making blue-
berry pie with the berries we picked yesterday morning in Richmond
(what is Richmond? wealthy world I told Alex): only a cock crowing
& the drone of a plane, bushes taller than we are, lushest bluest
berry in the shadow within, hair full of leaves & twigs, ears full
of chickens—I want to see the chickens, my shoe's undone, I don't
WANT these berries, let's go home: hot tears & dirt: depth of
summer.

They're reading books now in their pajamas, side by
side on the floor—dim resistance, mute chords, clouds mute even
them. It's coming (fall is), to the house. Down the mountain
houses will gather themselves. Build fires, burn rubbish, bake.
There's a damp wind blowing the curtain thru still-open windows,
thru . . .

sun cutting fog, falling on a piece of backyard, sun-
flowers. Those berries *offered* themselves in their nonchalance. no
worries. protected in the green there sun filters thru. to blueblack,
dusky, soft to touch, round crowns separating from stem, welled up.
This richness absorbed in the green, a fatness the whole bush exhibits:
summer

there is a being that doesn't question itself. Rubbing
elbows in the sun, bright as fly wings, But this fog that blankets,
soft, rot: signals a falling apart of things, leaves eaten away to
skeletal fly wings, & all the juices running elsewhere, a mad
exhilaration . . .

equals the singing that begins, open-mouth'd against
time: a chorus of late summer people, friends, at dusk singing the
dream they had gathered last night at the open door, singing wild

flowers gathered like summer in their hands, *against* my hurry singing
you don't have to hurry, it will all be here, as it always has been,
under the day's weather, whether you find us or not . . .

(& Michael
who has bought "blood, sweat, & tears,'" muffled as the morning sits
heavy sounds of baking, teasing, mind's annoyance, trucks, phone-
ringing, wants to know . . . I don't remember a single cut from the
side we played. It wasn't *that* singing but something that seemed to
rise & fall with the wind . . .

abandoned,
is the sound of wind
swinging thru open doors, holes, grass grown up withered, sere,
shaking its head against the planking. clouds cross. wind. is the
memory of voices' faded passion, passing, no more than wind?
Get off my foot, Alex is standing on my foot, he was reading a book
to me & now he's standing on my foot. Awkward, make-believe idiot
smile, does it hurt? does it really hurt? No more than wind than
the inexplicable changes. He was my friend! Dumdum, I'm mad at
you (for being? Tears. & everyone yells, get off his foot.

Why foot?
Why does he choose that? The smile lingers awkward, heavily out of
place. He *knows* it hurts but what does he want, the painful admission?
"throwing his weight around." I'm here, I'm here. It's a painful
self that wants to be with the rest of us who move more easily thru
each other. Or do we? Wanting love, needy, unable to love ourselves,
ashamed of the fathomless depths our need writes across our face.

I was in a hurry, afraid of being left behind, of not reaching you
before you left with them, for the canyon, canyons of the interior
where they, where we, were all going—these red landforms occupied by
fading sun. "Home is where the heart is," but if it's dark & the red
stream pumping out of these landlocked gorges falters, stopt, with
nowhere to go, no route we recognize as ours?

As outside, the unwanted
linger in outer doorways, in our awkward smiles that shut. We pass
them by, those gutted houses unoccupied by self, four sheets to the
wind, stumbling past & into the
shadows, or shadows of open doors.

They are not open. At the meeting's church-hall doors, people of
every hue from right to left press in, well-dressed, none of the
victims, none of the powerless. Whose power is it? Whose world?

Let the community decide what to do with gangs, Sabatino said, not
the police.

But then, there's always the chance encounter with a
bear, up the mountain, blueberry picking, we held our breath. He
shambled aimless around the bush, rearing up on his hind legs
suddenly surprised, graaar: a huge hole to fall into. nothingness.
We'd forgotten the bears, we forget they raid our garbage cans in
fall, coming down to us where the food is, where the house is
stocked from a rich summer (rows & rows of okanagan peaches in the
dusky basement, shining in glass jars . . .

Suddenly I'm outside—in the dark, crying. In anguish, hot tears,
the wind rustling around me might be anything on its way to get me
in this black place off the road I've stumbled to, I don't care,
let it come—the bears, murderers, whatever they are. Past caring,
so caught up in the pain of betrayal that breeds hot tears, a
thousand demonic thoughts that twist my heart, she doesn't care, they
don't love me (he has left me). She wants to drive me out of the
house, her house (wealthy world), as she has driven herself in a black
rage, a cloud of flies, a cloud of biting thoughts—I hate her,
hate her for having brought down all my trust for what it is, the
false dreams of any silly child.

The dog shifts on my foot, he doesn't
understand what we're doing at the end of a gravel road, bitter in
the dust, the moving leaves, the bush stretching back up a mountain
that doesn't register human passion— I'm beginning to smell the
leaves, wet leaves of night, remind me of how I can't (I won't) go
back, of the rotting apples in the backyard, phlox standing pink in
the unnatural light of kitchen windows streaming, into the dark
                                                          where,
invisible, nose blockt, I can't stop crying, hot with hurt & pent-up rage.
She doesn't understand the last thing in the world, the end of, a
hole, is that people are horrible (ursus horibilis) you can't trust
them— So you thought, you assumed, they wanted you. They didn't.
So you counted on it? We decided we don't want you to come. In the
end you don't count, you're out in the dark, outside the houses all
those real people you see are talking & walking in.

The party is there in the light. The party is where the power is
(the party in power?) Those who are there are party to power, know how
to lock you out to assert *their* place. Locked out, you're nowhere—
"I'm a dream in somebody's imagination"—mine.

No, I won't be out where
she is. I won't let them cut the ground from under me. She says this
isn't her country, she says we don't belong here. Where do I belong?
Now, right now, I belong in the dark & dust, with the trees . . .

A tremendous sighing in the wind that blows around us. These things
are silent like me, that is, they *cannot* speak. Yet feel, what they
feel, what I, what each . . . only their sensing, dark. Swallowed up
feet (no longer move) these, our not arms & feet simply, move toward
each other, tentative, looking, for some *you* out of the absence
night is, everywhere. & then wells up these leaves, this earth,
these berries blue and luscious into our hands, this wealthy world we
hold, only as it falls from us, at the turn, at the swallowing up
of summer into fall. So that here, at the edge of the world in a
time the bear abducts stray blueberry pickers, they return, charged
with so much power they give off heat to all, gathered in the dark
around a dancing fire, people: light struck, shine in the heat of it,
singing out of their time to you . . . to you . . .

                                    Winter (not-summer)
is cold, wild.

95

He has hewn, it is huge, a table out of wood, not solid wood but
timbers screwed together, bolted rather, he is learning to be a
shipwright & it rocks, this table, when we sit down to it, like
some awkward canoe, boarded by the weight of food & our own selves,
heavy with doubt, & leaping, shadows on the wall, at any insult,
careful to pass the food, dishes heaped with lentils, vegetables
& soup, all made by different hands, it is communal, but what do we
have in common? this suspicion, that all might share, suspicious that
all might not be here, equally present.

Here is a man who wields
heavy tools, here is one who huddles at a corner on a small stool.
& the children argue, where, where are their places, their rightful
places in this design? He objects to a child sitting at the head of
the table, he who shapes the very table we all sit to, but cannot
shape our relations. "More room, more room." "Your elbow's in my
plate." Or who is to sleep in the basement, who the upstairs, or
the room that is too small for one, where two can hardly find an
intimate space in this house which is breaking apart, creaking under
our various tensions, in a wind that is always creeping thru any
crack, tho we tape up the windows so that they will not open any
more.

What do we share but the wish to see right relation? It
cannot be imposed. In place of the given we seek territory. Masked
faces figure an account of who owes who. The grocery bill is taped
to the kitchen cupboard. She figures out each share, & is it fair
that some would rather eat meat while others drink expensive coffee
substitutes? Who will wash the floor next week?

And yet,
exhilaration in a dream communicates heat against the full moon's
white pure principle. "How do you see the house?" Over & over
the question is asked of each new initiate. A family, she says,
I want to bring my children into. A commitment & responsibility.
To share. A place to be with others, he says, singing & dancing.
I imagine the empty house at night, full moon, I imagine the yellow
eyes of a cavernous head we ourselves have filled with light. Night
of the arising of what we thought was dead. Rises up whole & huge:
possibility.

It's not ideology, he says, which justifies what actually happens between people. & she: I've always liked that quote from Marx, if the commune fails it's not the principle of the commune that is wrong.

Do people fail? I knew you would fail, he said, to love me enough. No one is loved, no one here. The table rocks, while outside a full moon rises, tainted with all that is negative, no exit, no vacancy, no trespassing. Stop: red: stop. "You are practising bourgeois idealism." Between the trees' frigid structure, above the skyline, a full moon rises into impossible white that clarifies all that is outside.

Trees & rocks. Know nothing. They take place to be, is, a taking place, as only in solitude I know, returning up the long dark road last night, out of the party & into the rain, see trees, finally, after walking miles wrapt in myself, see birch & maple glistening in a rainlight, listening, are, no one finally.

Is this dream a kind of taking? not to take but *fill* place. Listen. Writing in the large silence of a house filled with sleeping bodies upstairs & down, my own ghostly against the window pane, & outside, dripping still of early rain, these birches, luminous under moon & streetlamp, their mashed leaves clogging the road. Black, black is what we exist in, but for the dream our bodies dance, soft, ebb & flow of breath, touching, like the sea— "even sand," she said, "even sand & gravel are alive." As I did dance last night in the dream, in exhilaration like flight (wings, my dress), except that my feet beat out a very exact & complicated rhythm on the ground. Ground & air, water nearby (empty? lot or dock? an abandoned place where people had gathered, night, under the bridge, some kind of celebration of return—they were coming—who?) my dress, soaring like flames as I raised my arms in a continual burning & renewal, rooted to the ground or beaten-down dirt (floor). Brett tells me this morning he too dreamed, down in the basement of the house, so clearly he woke himself, of dancing, people dancing by water, connections of stars which kept exploding into further stars, & a sea which was pulled or receded to the mouth (river-running sea, they said the sea is a river running north) by these events.

our house is invaded, moon & tide become part of our lives because they are, taking place. Bob, telling us last night in the kitchen how the boat launching monday at the shipyard must be at full moon tide. Night. Sleep. He falls asleep across a beam with the hammer in his hand, this shipwright. Fragments. How do they cohere, except as chance encounters?

97

Is it by chance she lifts the light & sets love burning? By chance
that winter follows? in abandonment, a wandering through tasks that
set relation right. Winter, here, is a gathering.

                                        They take place,
as each of us, these starry explosions or chance encounters that
generate all possible lines of relation in this house. The collision
last night was a breaking down the wall, that membrane that separates
the paths we run on. "It's all water under the bridge," he said,
entering this house which, at the dead center of winter, at the mouth
of a sea where the sun goes down, opens suddenly into a well—"all
creatures therein." Through hell, through earth, into the open air
which offers, skyrocket, spring we wind our way among, organic
implosions of relationship, our lives.

from STEVESTON

Imagine: a town

Imagine a town running
                (smoothly?
a town running before a fire
canneries burning

              (do you see the shadow of charred stilts
on cool water? do you see enigmatic chance standing
just under the beam?

                He said they were playing cards in the
Chinese mess hall, he said it was dark (a hall? a shack.
they were all, crowded together on top of each other.
He said somebody accidentally knocked the oil lamp over, off
the edge

       where stilts are standing, Over the edge of the
dyke a river pours, uncalled for, unending:

                  where chance lurks
fishlike, shadows the underside of pilings, calling up his hall
the bodies of men & fish corpse piled on top of each other (residue
time is, the delta) rot, an endless waste the trucks of production
grind to juice, driving through

                smears, blood smears in the dark
dirt) this marshland silt no graveyard can exist in but water swills,
endlessly out of itself to the mouth

              ringed with residue, where
chance flicks his tail & swims, through.

Steveston as you find it:

　　　　　　　　　　　　　　multiplicity simply there: the physical matter of
the place (what matters) meaning, don't get theoretical now, the cannery.

It's been raining, or it's wet. Shines everywhere a slick on the surface of
things wet gumboots walk over, fish heads & other remnants of sub/ or
marine life, brought up from under. Reduced to the status of things hands
lop the fins off, behead, tail, tossed, this matter that doesn't matter,
into a vat or more correctly box the forklifts will move, where they swim,
flat of eye—deathless that meaningless stare, "fisheye" (is it only
dead we recognize them?) in a crimson sauce of their own blood.

　　　　　　　　　　　　　　　　　　　　　　　　　We orient
always toward the head, & eyes (éyes) as knowing, & knowing us, or what we do.
But these, this, is "harvest." These are the subhuman facets of life we the
town (& all that is urban, urbane, our glittering table service, our white
wine, the sauces we pickle it with, or ourselves), live off. These torsos.
& we throw the heads away. Or a truck passes by, loaded with offal for what
we also raise to kill, mink up the valley.

　　　　　　　　　　　　　　　　　That's not it. It's wet,
& there's a fish smell. There's a subhuman, sub/marine aura to things. The
cavernous "fresh fish" shed filled with water, with wet bodies of dead fish,
in thousands, wet aprons & gloves of warm bodies whose hands expertly trim,
cut, fillet, pack these bodies reduced to non-bodies, nonsensate food *these*
bodies ache from, feet in gumboots on wet cement, arms moving, hands, cold
blowing in from open doors facing the river, whose ears dull from, the in-
sensate noise of machinery, of forklifts, of grinding & washing, of conveyor
belt. Put on an extra sweater, wear long underwear against the damp that
creeps up from this asphalt, from this death that must be kept cool, fresh.

"DISINFECT YOUR GLOVES BEFORE RESUMING WORK"

That no other corpus work within it. Kept at the freshest, at the very point of
mutable life, diverting, into death. To be steamed in cans, or baked, frozen in
fillets, packaged sterile for the bacteria of living bodies to assimilate. break
down. Pacific Ocean flesh.

No, that's not it. There's a dailiness these lives revolve around, also immersed.
Shifts, from seven to four or otherwise. Half an hour for lunch. & a long
paperwrap & tied form outside the lunchroom, keeping cool. 'til shift's
end & the fridge, supper, bed. "my life," etc.

100

"You leave 2 minutes after 4,
& not before, you understand? Two minutes after." Two minutes, as if that,
together with the sardine cans for ashtray, made all the difference. Which is,
simply, as two Japanese women sit, relaxing with their fifteen minute coffee
out of thermos, more likely hot soup, one rearranges the chrysanthemums, red &
yellow, she placed in an empty can on their table this morning when the day
began. Or more directly how in "fresh fish" the lunchrooms, men's & women's,
face over an expanse of roof with flowerboxes even, river & the delta, Ladner,
space. & remain spacious, time turned calendar of kimona'd beauty, kneeling,
on the wall. While in the cannery close to wharfedge they face north,
backed by old wooden lockers to the door: DO NOT SPIT IN THE GARBAGE.
                                                                USE THE
TOILETS. & here they flood in together, giggling, rummaging thru bags,
eating grapes, girlish even ("I've worked here 20 years") under severe
green kerchief like Italian peasants, except that they are mostly Japanese,
plunked under a delicate mobile of Japanese ribbon fish in their gumboots
& socks. Break, from routine, with the ease of tired bodies laughing,
for what? "It's life." *Their* life?

                                  Or how the plant packs their lives, chopping
off the hours, contains *them* as it contains first aid, toilets, beds, the
vestige of a self-contained life in this small house back of the carpentry
shed, where two woodburners are littered with pots & hot plates, & the table
still bears its current pattern of dominoes. Where a nude on the wall glints
kittenish at one of the two small rooms inside, each with iron bed. Some
sleeping place between shifts? Dark. Housing wet dreams, pale beside the
clank of forklift, supply truck, welding shed.

It's a mis-step, this quiet gap on everyone else's shift, when you're off,
when accidental gravel rattles loud on the wooden walk. wan sun. coffee,
gone cold. There's a surface skin of the familiar, familial. Running into
shadow, where old socks, someone else's intimate things, call up the fishy
odour of cunt, of lamp black in the old days you could hear them screwing
behind their door (cardboard), & even the kitchen sill exists to pull you
back in, to smallness, a smell of coal, the aura of oil, of what comes up
from under, sleeping — nets, wet still from riverbottom, & the fish.

This darker seam that slips underneath the coppery gleam of all those cans stacked
flat after flat, waiting transfer. Men. & Women. Empty familiar lunchroom.
& the dream, pounding with the pound of machinery under mountains
                                                  of empty packer
pens at night, the endless (white) stream of flesh passing under the knives,
To be given up, gone, in a great bleeding jet, into that other (working) world.

101

trickle of broken hose. old netting, sacking, rope.
paint everywhere. penboards on end & painted silver. poles with
bells to be fitted, new springs & line. the sound of a boat
rubbing against tire, whisper of rope, shift across rope as a
boat lifts or falls.

Sea Trek, *Elma K*, *Miss Nikko 70*, ready,
day after day copper painted & caulked & overhauled, now they
wait, feeling that suck in green & oily shallows, feeling
afternoon leaf so close at hand, & late (derisive, clucking of
a gull domestic, finally) they wait, for headway out to the open
seas/ the open season, current, storm: & fish.

Finn Road

"Seems like, with men around, you're always at the stove."
Making cabbage rolls, something that keeps in a slow oven when
the boys come back, late, from fishing. It's her day off. She
went to town to pay the bills, "somebody's got to look after that."
But tomorrow she'll be up when the tide's full, at 3 or 4 in the
morning, down to Finn Slough where her boat's moored. Been out
fishing for 20 years now. And walks, from counter to stove, with a
roll.

It's a hot day, sultry, rain spit in the air.
There's cotton laid out on the kitchen table, a pattern. "Making
a housecoat," something cool to wear when it gets humid. Seems
like, whenever it's strawberry & haymaking time, there's rain.

Response

"I think the fish like their water clean too,"
she says with a dry laugh where: this outgoing
river, this incoming tide

                               mingle & meet. To take
no more than the requisite, *required* to grow, spawn,
catch, die: required to eat.

we'd house ourselves in, all this wind & rain.
Confuse us. Driving lines that shift, the floor does, ground or
under sea, to cast, at low tide what lies uncaught, uncovered
traces only, of sun & the moon's pull.

Unseen, how lines run
from place to place. How driving from town she follows the water's
push, the fields, drained by ditch to river to, the sea at,
where she lives . . . "At the end of the road," she says
Steveston is. At the mouth, where river runs under, in, to the
immanence of things.

To live in a place. Immanent. In
place. Yet to feel at sea. To come from elsewhere & then to discover
love, has a house & name. Has land. Is landed, under the swaying
trees which bend, so much in this wind like underwater weeds we think
self rises from.

But the place itself, mapt out, a web, was grass:
tall, bent grass swaying heavy with seed. Cottonwood whose
seeds make a web in the wind. "It was a wild place—where foxes
might live," this marsh persistent bending windswept lines of force,
current, men drag their nets thru to recover (as if they could)
wealth
fishy as quick slime, saying, it's here, & here, & here,
this self
whose wealth consists of what?

A house? built by
hands & handed down from father to not son but daughter, tenuous as
moonlight sometimes, hair so strong sun weaves ladders in it, webs,
of strange connection. Light & dark. And so from this place to
centre, dreaming of the source of things, flow, a ditch, from there to
. . . Japan & back? No, somehow love runs, shaken by the waters' pull
& leaves a network of men beached. Remembering now whose name,
in the dark the one owl calls & foxes' gloaming eyes, lit up by
the future (moon) say love, love will be . . . a fisherman's dream,
the web, the snare . . .

To retain, to remember, simply, the right names for things. Kneeling
by the bed, in a knotting of grass she seeks to see her life (oinari-san,
by the power of foxes) dreams: I found myself in a hall piled high with
dirty dishes, no one around, I had to wash them all. How they pile up,

these leftovers trapt, out of the flow. Like the fish. Like the
network of fishy familial parts these knots are, "my daughter, my house,"
these knots that bind.

                         At the end of the road, at the river's mouth,
muddy with all these empty dykes & misplaced hope she's removed herself,
disappearing like foxes of the past into the underbrush, whose wall's
this briar hall of moonlight, whisper of old rituals: who are you now
you've cut yourself adrift, alone?

                                        "I'm not really in
the Japanese community, I don't belong to Buddhist Church, I don't
send my kids to sunday school."

Who also, neither north or south, drives back, late, by the shining
watery roads from town, from the Western Front, from the centre of things,
to mud & drainage ditch, familiar house, shit, the accumulation of
personal things. To the place of firstcomers where a woman felt
"like I was living in a wild field," where the grass, where the lines of
wind, where the lines of power moved clear in a field of power.

                            Where now her house stands
webbed with weaving, leaf tracery & light (of pots, plants), a house she
inhabits, immanent, at the edge of town a field they're raising houses on.
And coming from town, driving down by the scummy & soontobecovered ditches
(remnant, of leftover rains, plucked cabbages in the sun, & wind) where do you
find her, out?
            as now by day,
                        or in, summer's wilder growth, around &
past (the stepping stones at back are wood & cut by hand) amidst (there is
no closer) hands full of beans & fingers in the heart of, "well I *live* here,"
lettuce, children, friends, you find a self, under the trees that sway like
underwater weeds, connecting things.

Steveston, B.C.

Steveston: delta, mouth of the Fraser where the river empties, sandbank after
sandbank, into a muddy Gulf.

Steveston: onetime cannery boomtown: "salmon capital of the world": fortunes
made & lost on the homing instinct of salmon.

Steveston: home to 2,000 Japanese, "slaves of the company": stript of all their
belongings, sent to camps in the interior away from the sea, wartime, who
gradually drift back in the '40's, few who even buy back their old homes,
at inflated prices, now owning modern ranchstyle etc., & their wives,
working the cannery, have seniority now, located.

Steveston: hometown still for some, a story: of belonging (or is it continuing?
lost, over & over . . .

          Steveston divided into lots with an ox
barbecue, sold the lot but only bit by bit Steveston belongs to its temporal
landowners & those who, Packers & Nelson Brothers, Canadian Fish, hold chunks of
the waterfront like gaps (teeth) of private territory, "use at your own risk,"
but the shark (with his teeth dear) speculates, brooding on housing developments
whose sidewalks pave over the dyke, whose street lamps obliterate the shadow
bowl of night on Lum Poy's field, west, & south, as the geese fly past the old
Steves place & on, to dark to
          wherever fish come from, circling back in
to their source:

        We obscure it with what we pour on these waters, fuel, paint, fill,
the feeding line linking us to Japan & back, wherever, cargo ships, freighters
steam up river & only the backwaters house these small boats whose owners,
displaced & now relocated as fishermen can be, fishing up nets full of shadow/
food for the canneries to pack, blip blip sonar & even these underwater
migrations visible now as routes, roots, the river roots, out from under

                brail net
they lift these fishes with, reading a river gulf, Or, visibly

how it pours, this river, right over the top of the rock dam into Cannery Channel swirling freshet on & right on past the sedge that roots sediment, witness these gaptoothed monument pilings, pile stumps of ghostly canneries settle, into obscurity (a map necessary, or key, to the old locations) locating thus (where are we?) shipwreck, a rusty wheel, a drum, inarticulate emblems of this life craft that runs, that continues, this busy work of upkeep (*without* us) wheeling its river bank into sun, into the blind anonymity of sea light, the open

sun. a sea men sink their lives into, continue, dazzlingly undeciphered, unread days, dazed with the simple continuance of water pour, of wind, of small stores turning their annual credit ledgers, debit, silent as winter falls, falls, pours.

This is the story of a town, these are the people, whose history locates inside of dream, in site of (in situ) down by the riverbank a torrent pouring past its sloughs & back channels, boat basins time repeats, this one was Phoenix, this one Atlas, or leaving Hong Wong/Wo's obliterated letters, even whole names along with bits of crockery water washes, dead dogs, web caught up under the shadows of these buildings men would cast, like nets of retrieval, only to cast their names across the line that water washes, away, incessant, swollen, by reaches of the sea our lives respond to, irresistibly drawn, these precarious floats, boats equipt with the latest machinery, radar, sonic scan, drifting, limbs extended, sometimes logs & deadheads, sometime creatures of motive that swim, *against* the source, but always continuing to return, always these lovely & perilous bodies drifting in spawn, swarm on out to sea.

from ZÓCALO

'Among the Aztecs dream interpretation &
divination by dreams were the prerogative
of the priestly class 'teopexqui,' the Masters of
the Secret Things; and among the Maya of
'cocome,' the Listeners.'

Dreams: Visions of the Night

Journey

They had come from elsewhere, hundreds of them. Now they are
stopped in a line that curves back down the road in the fading light.
She can see his white truck glimmering behind her, and behind him,
these cars, these trucks and jeeps and vans, sprawling into dark. Now
they are here, now she sees the actual lineup, sees she is in it, she feels
they have been pulled here, through a vast network of highways, roads,
to this, this centre (as if it were the heart of a continent, it isn't), this
inspection centre—yes, isn't that why they have come? the vehicles,
their mechanism requiring inspection.
                                        She takes her foot off the clutch
and rolls down the window. After flying through the passes of those
hills and then what seemed to be growing desert, though here, yes,
there are trees, but stunted and far apart—it's hard to adjust to a
crawl, her body, the car even, still canted forward in the impetus of
speed, flying, it felt like flying, both windows down, hair streaming
in the stream of air brushing her eyes, trying to gauge, by feel, the
lengths to leave according to their speed, his truck and her car juggling
position in a kind of follow the leader or, since both love speed, a kind
of dare, contingent on the bends, the turns, and then, after the tension
of thrusting ahead, letting her foot relax on the pedal, slipping back,
feeling the slippage of air over the body of her car which responds like
some animal alive to pavement its wheels mediate. Surrounding country,
then, was just a blur.
                      And now she is here, is in it, rolls down the
window and night comes in, just the beginning edges of it dawning

(how can that be?—but nothing seems to end here, sun glimmers horizontal and dusty behind those hills, as it has for the past hour, caught, on the verge of going—only not, only night bent on presence, invisibly growing.

And are they stopped? It seems to be something between first gear and none, or out of, slipping the clutch. Of course they're moving up a slight incline. Let the car ahead gain a few feet so at least she can *move* then, instead of slipping slipping the clutch. She misses their game and thinks he'll wonder what is holding them up. Glancing in the mirror for *him* now, and not the truck, she finds him a yard or so behind, arms crossed on the wheel and glancing out the side window. What's he looking at?

Rolls down hers, sees dust has stopped for the most part, just a light density in air, powder soft. Of course the earth here's sandy, or, she can't tell by colour, it's getting dark, it feels in the air, on the skin like a fine pulverized dirt, inland and old. The sea is beyond those hills, quite a long way beyond—was it yesterday? But there's a kind of freshness here she hasn't sensed before, not fresh, no, something out of night falling, some bush or herb that, freshened by the drop in temperature, releases an odour that is acrid and sweet.

She glances back at the truck, turning her head to look over her shoulder through the rear window. His window is dusty, he has the wipers going, squirting a clear arc to see through. She waves her hand to break his focus. He sees her and waves back and she turns forward, feeling a smile on her own face. Sees the car ahead has moved several yards. Shifts quickly into gear and follows. The smile, once she has felt it, begins to fade—it seems absurd to be smiling at a long line of cars —but she feels his presence warm behind her head like hair.

Near the top of the incline all the cars bear signs as if they had been numbered. She assumes she also has one and sees, glancing back, that he does too, but she doesn't remember seeing any men or feeling anyone approach the car. Maybe the signs have suction cups that would have been silently attached? Though she stares hard at the car ahead—actually it's a truck and, now that she stares intently, seems to be in some way official, a patrol truck, the kind a road construction crew uses to lead a line of cars through a restricted area—she cannot make out how the sign sticks. Each sign bears a number and a line or two of print too small to read. Not even the letters look recognizable and she thinks perhaps it's in some native language.

But now the truck in front, what is it doing? backs up a bit, turning, leaves the line and heads off down the road. Its brake lights flash on, pause, it is waiting—for her? Is she supposed to follow? If it's a patrol truck maybe it's starting a new lineup closer in to town, just to speed things up. She glances through the mirror, behind, to him, but can't make out whether he signals she should go or not. The patrol truck is still waiting, lights above and beside its sign flashing number seven. She's the next one, no one can move if she doesn't. She releases the clutch, steps on the pedal and veers out.

Her guide begins to pick up speed and she can see an unaccountable bend coming up. She glances back—is he following in the white truck?—she *thought* she saw something white, but her attention is taken up with manoeuvering the turn at high speed. Out in the open, now they have left the avenue and moved into open country, the truck is streaking down the road. She presses hard on the pedal trying to catch up but the distance lengthens. Is it trying to lose her? Should she have followed? She remembers getting out of the car to look at her sign. Was it number six? (at least she thinks she remembers) was it number nine? Yes, she had to fix it with the print so she could tell—it was number six. If the truck is number seven she must obviously follow it. But was it really part of the line? She sees in the growing distance a number of tail-dragging black sedans, she can almost hear shouts, dogs barking, can almost see the sedans full of people, kids. So it's a native truck, it has nothing to do with the line. But it must know where to go, it must be going somewhere. The dust it leaves fills up the road. Impossible, impossible to see. She comes to a halt beside a ditch filled with dry weeds, fencepost above, a field. No one else on the road. A creeping stillness that is twilight glimmers down its length.

She gets out and stands alone for some time. No one, nothing comes. The pavement through the soles of her runners where heat is trapped around her feet, a sweat that is even now turning cold in the cool of evening, the pavement feels smooth, hardly tangible. She moves off toward the edge where weeds are and dirt. Her walking has slowed to an effort through air thick with smells of, what, some kind of dry grass smoke. Distance is charged with it. A faint magnetism runs between things, the fencepost and her feet, this stalk and that. No moon? She has turned, intending the full horizon, but finds herself looking west to the hills light still flares behind.

She will go in, there is a driveway further back, much overgrown, she will go in and ask.

Their faces hang in the dusk like fruit off a tree. She is standing on their land talking to them. On her left a man bends slightly over a stick or the handle of a pitchfork. To her right the two women and the girl—their faces float up towards her in the dusk, hardly aware, it seems, of what she sees as startling: daughter, mother, grandmother clustered together like so many berries on the one bush—all staring, simply, at her own white face.

It was number seven, she says, the

truck, where would a number seven truck be going? You see, I'm number six and I was supposed to be following . . . and then she hesitates. If she is six, shouldn't the truck have been five since it was ahead of her? She remembers the number seven, seven, flashing in the light. But how could that be?

In the stillness they watch her face. Something is gathering in the air, something she can't see. 'Strange things . . .' He seems reluctant to go on, and she turns to the woman she imagines might speak out of sympathy. What does he mean?

The woman doesn't answer. Or rather, behind her a fence post comes into view, bearing something nailed to it, some flayed animal. Its tawny hide flares up in the halflight. Matted fur. A warning? She thinks, that skin was nailed there for someone to see.

'I will tell you now is the time, now, when man's powers are coming to the full . . .' It is pronounced, not spoken personally, not spoken to her at all. And yet she is allowed to overhear.

What do you mean? Is that all she can say? In the pressure of their silence she feels they feel she must know and is only pretending ignorance.

'The power of the sea and the power of dwarfs are acting together—that's what my mother would say.' She turns her head to the old woman but the woman continues staring at her without expression, without understanding.

Go back to the line, he says, we can't help you.

Walking back to the car she is walking *toward* the hills light is still fading behind. Time seems to press in from there, like some tide rising, like fear. He is right. They cannot help her.

Back in the car, she must turn around, but where? Drives on a little way, looking. There on the left, an abandoned garage, nailed shut, empty, and in front, a white truck. As she walks over to its window, she sees him in the passenger's seat, inert. For a second she thinks he is dead. What're you doing? Relief and fear sharpen her voice as he turns. He says quietly, I can't drive, and indicates the seat beside him. On it, a parcel trussed up in rope sits in front of the driver's wheel, bulkily in front, leaving no room for him.

I followed you when you first left the line, he says, I trusted your sense of direction. I thought you were following the sea.

Here? But then she remembers what was said. The parcel sits there, malevolent and unmoving. It almost emanates its own presence, not a sign but, more inexplicably, a knowledge of itself in front of them. She doesn't ask him how it got there.

We must go back. Now.

She is
driving and he is in her car. She is trying to explain that there is no
other way out but the way they came, that the country surrounds them
and there is very little room—only the thread of their coming the way
they came. They are still looking for a place to turn. Up ahead, a stone
wall on the right, and beyond it, a driveway. As the wall approaches
and runs beside them, he leans forward and she hears him say, they
knew how to depict expression, certainly—almost real. Looking, she
sees them rise up from the ground, a few lopsided crosses among them,
huge iron heads like jack-o-lanterns with holes for eyes and nose,
but the mouths have teeth, lips, some with tongues even, myriad
expressions of laughter, or scorn, or knowing smiles. As the car begins
to pick up speed, she sees, their lips parted slightly, they are breathing,
these mouths, as they themselves are turning into, a mistake, that
driveway, carried by the momentum of a plan, in to the driveway
of those others, those heads, too late, onto *their* ground—No!—
unwinds,

backward,

they are flying backward outside time in open
country, across fields, across terrain that slips under them as they
fly back in the slippage of their own coming, down the road,
through,

she sees him in a corner on a chair, unblinking, his stare
which hasn't left her face since she walked away, the man she asked
directions of, she sees he has known, he has always known, having just
removed the pipe, it is in his hand, it gleams in his eye which holds
hers as they fly by, just before and into the night, she realizes, looking
back, how small he is.

Donde esta las damas? taking the secondclass bus to Uxmal & having
to use the secondclass waiting room, where the washroom's locked,
or what she thinks is, name fallen off the door. & he points, just
points, with a supreme indifference. Does she say it then so awkwardly?
or does he know that when he speaks her eyes will go blank, panic,
she has forgotten every spanish word she ever knew. But he points to
the door which is the one she tried, & she says no, & someone else
explains it's closed, cerrado, o & she was right it wasn't just a broom
closet but where can she go? & they tell her to go round & over into
the firstclass waiting room—official sanction then? But the bus is
ready to leave & has he climbed aboard, the driver she last saw leaning
against his vehicle with those other casual & confident stars of the
depot? When he climbs aboard the show's begun & waits for no
insignificant passenger in the washroom, who will not be missed (except
by Yo, & he can't speak spanish). It's a three-hour busride, even if she
can't shit yet—well, that's the actual reason, isn't it, hoping the large
jugo de naranja would do it, no more coffee no, racing back through
the waiting room, past the guard (don't stop me), & into the potent
smell of piss & shit (an air, phew), plastic buckets beside each stool
filled with stained bits of paper, everyone's variety: newspaper, toilet
paper hoarded in purses, pages torn from magazines, extravagant
kleenex, & the stinking remains of individual bodies passing through
in time. She is too pressured by & tries to remember the seller of hot
tamales squatting outside the depot doors, already, early morning, on
spitstained, littered, & no doubt pissedon cement (is that where they
go? who live on the street in the public wind & sun) their day all day
before them, children threading dribbled mazes in the empty fountain.
'You have to have a ticket to use this washroom.' (Where *do* they go?)
But it's no good, she can't imagine herself bodily into that woman
squatting on the step, she can't imagine her day, its ease (or un-ease),
as she walks back to the bus, wondering now where does it go, all that
water & its contents, into what septic tank that doesn't process toilet
paper?

Yo too is tense, same problem—any luck? no—as the bus
driver swings into his seat with manifest definition, his partner nods,
the door swings shut & they back out into the yard. This is the first
bus they've taken with no shrine above the windshield, but he's very
good, their driver, manoeuvering the long body of his vehicle at just
the right angle to make those narrow turns, diagonal, honking their
way through stone streets & out into the main road, into highway,
sun (streaming everywhere), & fleetly past the pepsi bottling plants,
the airport maintenance sheds. Travelling west or south? The map, a
little one in the guidebook, shows only the road threading page top to

page bottom, marked with a pyramid, Uxmal, pirámide: it surprised her, that word, made it sound more esoteric than the terrain they were passing through could possibly lead to—possibly? pirámide: outcome. & where are they? She looks for the sun past his arm that stretches up to the baggage rack, braced against the movement of the bus. Discomfort: a falling apart. What can she tell him? to relax? that the body will look after itself, that she's long since given up trying to control its vagaries (has she? racing through the waiting room) & moreover how does she know what his must feel like, to him, what its importunities might be?

At any rate, the maguey fields keep rolling by, whole fields dry, & even the maguey dusty looking in the heat—'all of it one living rock (living?) . . . has wonderfully little earth,' this shelf, 'limestones risen from the sea.' & she could tell him that too but it is also unnecessary. Morning, no breakfast, & the coming awake a difficult entry into the world, each at their own pace. Their bodies in fact are here together, in this continuing suspension of them all in swaying space. Light streams in from their side (which means, south? she'll never get it straight, each time they turn, land turns) onto their hands, his arm, & there is nothing to do but continue, like the morning, to some unknown place.

But the moment she sees them she sees Yo has been watching all along, they are so vividly present: he whitehaired & erect, in his seventies maybe, she with a long grey braid down her back, stiller in her expansive flesh. They sit two rows up & across the aisle, as if they were attending some extraordinary event. Now he leans over to question a woman opposite about Campeche—that is the only word she catches, Campeche. Yes, the woman smiles, adds something, ah, he leans back & so informs his wife who nods of course, they had boarded the bus that said Campeche, hadn't they? You make sure you are on the right bus, that's all, but even the name, even the way he says it, 'Campeche,' disbelieving, & the fierce attention of his back, suggest he knows this bus, suspiciously like any other, is taking them away. Now he explains & she listening, it is the way she is listening, not looking at him: he must explain, although she already understands, & the skin of her face finely lined, one bloodshot eye, turns to him, with sudden piercing assent, then away, soft wrinkled cheek again, a listening ear.

Marriage, she gestures at them, marriage is really a buddy system. Buddy? His eyes are caught by the women climbing on, baskets & children. It's what they use at children's camp when you go swimming, you always go out with a buddy, someone who keeps track of you—that way you can't disappear without anyone knowing.

He looks at her & she wonders what she said. Not the buddy system, perhaps, but the world, a swallowing. One mis-step & into . . .

I mean——(to him they may look quite otherwise)——I mean, if one of us disappeared no one else would mind, we're only passing faces. We're passing faces all the time, he quips, & aren't they remarkable? That isn't what she meant, as he knows, & she knows he is choosing not to respond so that what she meant fades under the sun lying on their arms, the camera lying on his lap, & in his eyes, these women & children: yes, she thinks, as she looks, their flower-embroidered (hui-huipils, even the sound, weeps like a small bird) flesh, blooming giggles & quick smiles——one, a child, sending curious glances at them from around a sheltering thigh, to whom she decides to smile & who, before she turns to hide her face, suddenly opens, blackeyed, woman-to-be already figured in that luminous look.

After Muna's thronged plaza where the women descend, the bus chokes a little as it leaves the houses, gearing down for the hills, Puuc. Staring at the map, trying to see hills on it, or read those alien names——Xtepen, Yaxopoil——is it Uksmal? Ukhmal? Ushmal? ('thrice-built,' how can she know that & not know how to speak it?) she might have missed the first sight had he not nudged her, look over there. From a mass of treetops it heaves up out of the terrain, dark in places, stone, yet manmade, wrought, & that, rising above the thorny trees, is what impresses her most, its old familiarity.

A european girl in shorts hoists her pack as the bus pauses, others rise, this must be it he says, stepping down into the full meridian of sun, exhaust fumes as the long body of the bus, o she forgot to catch their faces, slides past, taking the old couple with it.

They follow other tourists up the trail to a gate, a government sign, various do's & don'ts in spanish & english. While the ticket seller waits patiently for the right combination of pesos, a water tower on top of a house labelled 'reconstruction crew' leaks continuously down one wall——no one's home or they've laid off for the tourist season. Hot, hot, as the lingering touch of morning gives way to the weight of noon——& going without breakfast doesn't help, he says, eyeing the shacks with pepsi coolers, guidebooks under glass, i've got to get something to eat. It looms behind them, that mass of stone they haven't yet confronted, even as she is caught by his 'got to'——how're you feeling? seeing him suddenly dwarfed by it, herself too, you all right? his grim, fine, i'll get two pepsis, resisting the way it towers up into the blue, above them.

So that, sipping pepsis, sitting on the rocks that ring, parklike in the dust, some tree, she feels herself back off, even as they face it. Even from here, from the cigarettes & pepsi taste, people standing or walking (all those stones), even from the vantage point of paying patrons to a long dead show, it rises peculiarly human (what's inside? some child asks. rubble fill. what's rubble? stone

115

rubbish, is that all?) The guidebook says there are five temples, three of them buried inside, three levels, five successive houses of divinity —but what—'superimposed' the book says, facades, masks, frieze, inclined slopes—led to the building of this off-oval, two-layer mound, smooth & round as some child's sand castle, incredibly heaped to the sun?

It's called the Pyramid of the Magician, she says, as they watch two mexican boys start climbing, hauling themselves up its safety chain like humpbacked dwarfs (& how did they get the stones up? she imagines an enfilade of miniatures all toiling up its steep face, the cost of religion someone had said). According to the legend he was a dwarf (& why is she caught by that?) Aren't dwarfs always magicians? Yo asks, setting the empty pepsi down against a rock, his voice seeming to come from far off, disinterested, just as one of the boys starts to run, side to side in zigzag motion, that ends suddenly as he disappears into a cavity halfway up.

It's such a strange story, she persists, ignoring his attempt to confound dwarfs & magicians. But there is something about the day that gets in the way of their speaking to each other. It begins with a dwarf whose mother was a witch & hatched him out of an egg (so far back in time it can't even be told with any probity). She sent him off to challenge the king & the king said build a palace overnight or I'll kill you. His mother helped of course with magic (impossible, faced with the actual mass of stone where the second boy, still clinging to the chain, is looking around for his friend who emerges, beckoning to him, & they both disappear). So the next test the king demanded was one of endurance, that they should each drop very hard nuts on their heads, the dwarf of course to go first. The witch made a magic plate for the dwarf so he survived but when the king tried it he split open his skull. So the dwarf got to be king of Uxmal & she went off to live with a serpent in a waterhole.

Well, so she was the magician, he said, looking through his camera at the pyramid. (Was she? was that why they called the sculpture they took from the first temple Queen of Uxmal, even though it showed a man's head emerging from the jaws of a snake?) But it was the men who had all the power, it was the men who were priests here, & kings, & warriors. They wouldn't name the pyramid after a woman. Why not?

They didn't even have a goddess creator & destroyer, she was going to say, but when she looked at him his face was closed & unreadable, bent to the camera on which he was changing the lens, & she realized it wasn't information got from books she felt he was challenging but her sense of reality. Besides, these were spanish names they were arguing over, these buildings long abandoned, their original names lost in the trees that had grown up all around & through them by the time they were found.

& she suddenly thought: we will miss it, caught up in our heads, in our cameras & guidebooks, we will miss what we came for. I'm going to climb it. Go ahead.

        & so, flinging herself into the climbing, hands to the chain, feet to the steps—awkward, too steep & shallow to walk up erect, not stairs but steps, not made for walking, for what then?—she straightens up halfway & enters the cave. At once a darkness surrounds her, visceral in its smell of dank stone turned inward from the day, unlit for centuries, & the very present odour of human piss, of well-used secret places, as if she has entered the bodily cavity of some huge stone being. She feels a panic, a feeling of suffocation in the unreadable dark, & remembers the guide book had said 'you will need a flashlight.' So much for the hidden temple then. Continuing up the safety chain outside in the glaring light, she wonders what it is that pulls her toward a dark she can't read or (since the chain is set so low it's useless, & she straightens, holding her breath, a little nervous, fearing to look back at the steep ascent, & down, into all that shining space he sits at the bottom of, legs crossed under the shade of a tree, perhaps watching her, more likely picturing all their movements, these small figures crawling up the oval stone body of this giant, its contour surely female) —is it the disparity of act & legend, the slow historical process of this place built stage by stage by men toiling in the light of day—& the legend of its creation overnight by a woman, out of a spell?

        Almost at the top, open to the sky, she hears the guard's whistle, shouts, 'bájo, bájo,' directed at whom? Norteamericano, barefoot in cutoffs, climbing over what's left of the roof. He's telling you to get down, someone calls. Why? You're not supposed to climb on the roof, didn't you see the sign? I don't read signs that aren't in english. Heady with his own elevation, there at the top, one young man standing on a mass of stone, dwarfed by it. But reaching the top after his sullen descent, she understands: close to the sun, at its zenith, noon, anyone standing here, as one could not on the way up (steps, steps of the sun?) stands aloft over a world that stretches all around, north, south, east, trees they were sitting under all pelt & growth of rolling bush that hides this limestone shelf, hills, risen from the bottom of the sea, sea itself only infinite borders of consciousness at those corners earth folds into sky.

    It's silent on the roof of the world. Its steepness impels her to give up clinging to an earth that lies far below, to jump off, into the light & wind, the very heart of space—she recognizes as falling, as earth calling her back to itself—& shrinking, edges around a broken wall to the western face of the pyramid.

        There before her lies the full extent of Uxmal, its white-rose stone gleaming in a quadrilateral grace lifting stained friezes in walls, in combs, an undulation of planes & dark

heights crowned with trees, jungle she'd heard it called, that makes
the place itself a transformation of earth. Climbing over serpent heads
(one to sit on, like a throne) or down high steps, she turns to look up
at the ornate face of the temple, its doorway, someone posing stands,
just inside a mouth, heavily incised eyes above a jutting nose. The
camera, she thinks, would catch that mouth, that man standing in front
of its darkness there, but the face so huge, how far down would she
have to step to get it all?

    Wait, one of a pair of girls appears above the
step below, I can't believe how steep these stairs are. Both rise into view,
in jeans, walking shoes, nylon packs on their backs, to sink down onto
the top step with a smile at her, the smile of outsiders who recognize
their shared alienness. She could almost be sure, you're canadian?, but
only asks, where are you from? Calgary, we took the train down from
Palenque—had a great trip. They've traipsed all through the site,
without a guidebook, fascinated, even to the crumbled ruin on the far
hill. Prairie girls. Anything worth going over for? Well, there are caves.
Caves? Yes, caves in the ground, you know—(she feels a drop, a slight
tremor), it's a fantastic place really—do you know what these masks
are all about? Does anyone, she thinks, except for their surface, faces to
climb, sand castles in the wild. They're faces of Chac, she names him,
the rain god.

    And continuing her descent, wonders, *under* the name?
dry land, no water anywhere, but caves, caves. Somehow the witch
persists, chaotic mother, though all the images are male, Chacs, Bacabs
at the four corners, all ordered under the sun, all countable.

             She sees
him threading his way between carved & toppled stones ahead, faces,
remnant of the pyramid & its surrounding temples. He has been taking
pictures, she can tell by the way he walks, lightly, as if prepared to be
caught, eye caught, stopt. She hurries to catch up, his shoulder blades
under the white t-shirt a radiant thinness in the heat she would put
her arm around. Yo. Yoshio. He turns, how was it? I met two Calgary
girls, she laughs, jubilant now, they said there were caves. You climbed
to the top of a pyramid to find out about caves? She grins, abashed,
where else? He points to a line of people in the distance toiling toward
some building (palace? so the Spanish says), &, as they watch white
calves flash in the sun as knee after knee under leder hosen lifts over
the same stone, it'd make a fine movie, he admires, Seeing the Ruins.
That's not seeing the ruins. Too quick, wanting it to be something else,
always. He glances at her, she had missed the humour, & then at the
sun directly above them now—the day is getting on—& moves, while
she, pursuing that image of a cave (what is it about stone?) fights off
what is everywhere present, when that is all that is required, assuming
his steps on the narrow trail through rock: only to follow the trail
their steps unwind,

only to see how these buildings they have gained
front each other across a courtyard grass withers, under the heat,
a string of tourists passing through, colours like brief flowers, &
everyone's eyes on the dazzle of incised line against the light.
                                                                    An
exhilaration, this stone, these great dark doorways whose lintels, like
steps of the pyramid, must be climbed—hand up, a hoist. He stations
himself for a good perspective on the corner building with its columns
& serpents, & she steps inside, into a strangely shallow room. It rises
upward like a vault, no windows, only this massive stone exuding damp
& mould in a downward displacement through air, of its own weight,
wrought, against itself, into this arching slope. She tries the next, &
the next, all of them alike, all vaults, all windowless, & he enters, asks,
what could they have been for? no one could live here.
                                                            Already, seeing
him come in from the day, his white shirt bright against his face that
is always darker, eyes full of the shine of lens & light, she sees the
polychrome image he presents, vivid. He glances around then throws
out, burial chamber? The door's too big. She's seeing him framed there,
one hand cradling his camera (what he will *make* of it), the other in a
back pocket twists his body, single & resistant in the doorway there,
the better to see. Man, she thinks, men with their distancing eye. She
feels a pang of envy for that clarity, & leaning forward, you're standing
in the light you know, bites his ear. As his hands disengage themselves
to enclose her, she sees over his shoulder the grassy courtyard their
cave looks out on & the small figures of all the others. So you've found
a use for it (his teasing tries to meet her), & in The Nunnery too. She
wants to say they didn't have nuns, but doesn't. His body feels warm
& resilient against her skin already chill from the mould. Do you think
these rooms were here for their doorways? she murmurs into his neck.
Are we in one? he asks, withdrawing, & she thinks he feels framed.
I'm trying to seduce you. You're playing with the idea of being a nun.
But there weren't nuns here! Nevertheless—he grins, you're irrevocably
christian.
                    Astonished, she walks out into the light & follows him down
the steps into the heart of the quadrangle. Is she trying to read these
stones with christian eyes? what does she or he or anyone take from
them? Except a profound sense of order, of an order that once made
sense, wholly sufficient to itself, the coming & going of sun & moon
& venus tracked with human eyes & plotted in immense recognitions—
fogotten now, or somehow mutely present? Do you want to use the
camera, he asks, offering her what he is here for. No, she waves the
guidebook, I'll stick with this.
                        Having walked through the ballcourt
whose walls have left only grassy inclines & broken rings ("cannot be
interpreted properly"), held up by two elderly ladies of a party

stumbling up the tumbled bank of a massive ruin ('although badly destroyed . . . the remains prove that'), they divert to follow a path though grasses & thorn bushes to a tessellated structure called The Dovecote. It towers above them, lacy stonework crest of square holes sun plays through, all if it leaning crazily toward them out of the blue. Having drained his visual curiosity, he lays the camera aside & lies down in the grass. Aren't you going to walk through that arch? vaulted like the rooms below, but leading onto bush, a genuine passageway. No, I've had enough. I'm just going to see where it goes. He nods.

When she turns, having walked through, she turns, she has come through to the other side of the site, these broken open vaults exposed to sky, it is onesided this Casa de Palomas (where are the birds?) it is a false front filled with holes & she has walked through into what lies behind the scene, *escena*, sheltered place. What lies behind the scene is bush, a jungle of trees, grasses, cactus, none she can name, a thicket the small path finds its way amid, into a dip, hollow, & then, towards the sky, she lifts her eyes, another hill, all stony, oddly treed, no hill, a mound. And suddenly she is in the midst of an immense plaza, for there, surrounding her, rise ridges that are not ridges, trees grown out of fallen buildings, an ancient square, contrived & once inhabited, lost now, giving up to hidden urges of nature, growth sprouting everywhere. They who knew the steps of the sun & moon, the steps of the year, who knew how to count backwards a hundred thousand years—did they who knew the beginnings, know this?

No one else around, & the path leads into a hollow, into the depths of day, heat, the stirring of foreign leaves on foreign trees, a conspiracy of insects. She is afraid but the path says come on. One is a visible number & she feels very visible walking down the path, she shuffles her feet, she makes a noise for the snakes to hear, so they can get out of her way—although she knows it isn't her way but theirs. The ruin, in all its monumental silence, says nothing to her, only stands, stands at the edge of an earth she descends, she chooses, between two paths, she keeps her eye on the mound as best she can, through the increasing foliage. And then as the path turns at the bottom of the hollow, across & to one side she sees a hole. Powdery white limestone opens on the dark, mouth— enough room for one person to slip into, lowering herself down.

She thinks of the Calgary girls. She remembers their enthusiasm, imagines a flashlight, rope. She thinks of limestone, of how it's given to crack, of how it sinks. She thinks of snakes. She thinks of the men who were priests, & the dark intensifies, a hole that recedes into earth pulling her with it, sun swallowed up by night where those underground mock those who would come, aha you have stepped out of place, you have stepped out of time, you will lose your face . . .

120

No, that is another story having to do with men who are gods. Her feet are on the path & the ruin lies ahead but she no longer wants to go there. The end of the story, she thinks, I didn't tell him how the witch exchanges water for children she feeds to the serpent. That is a sacrifice she can't understand & struggles away from. Perhaps he is right, she wants her individual soul—'irrevocably christian' after all.

She hurries back— feet send little stones skittering down the ascent, little puffs of dust —she reaches the crest, the arch & through: he is still there, both hands curled under his cheek, knees drawn up, lying old & foetal like a dwarf fallen freshly asleep on the skin of the earth.

Merida

On the other side of the square, they are, we are, he is saying, on the
side of the square we never sit on, morning, swallows the zócalo,
filled with it, that light ease light pours, into at centre (hole), pole they
are taking the xmas tree down, no more lights, daytime dead outline
of what was, at night, a coloured fantasy, but the tinsel wreaths still
swing, looping across paths that ray out from that spot their eyes are
fixed on, still, he is right, we are, on the side we never sit on, & though
morning swallows, in its light space freshening of day, all that night
lets run, strange currents, vampire bats at the movie house, or the
laughing seductive strays, giving way to the world, teenage derelicts
at midnight play around the original derelict himself swept, even he
swept out by morning, its shallows, leaving them all a little beached,
the paltry litter of yesterday, light raying through the indian laurel,
their old trunks' tatter whitewash adrift in peels the balloon man
goes slowly by, trailing pinks & blues, through a trickle of hose,
someone's watering, halfhearted, gone off for coffee, gone off into the
morning scatter through the day, knowing, even the gardener knows,
how one must splay out, simply, to be here & not—it's not the zócalo,
it's not the morning swallowing, it's night, under the o so solid scatter
of these pavingstones, dark clings, & she must not, step into that
house again—

        did you see him, she says (can you keep me here?) the
shoeshine man on the other side of the square, we must have passed
him, on our way here, though she had actually forgotten to look. No,
he says, I didn't, but the blind man's there, & she could see him
inching his way along the wall to change position, all day with his
hand out, blind faith, not the scrawnier hand of the dwarf woman in
the sidestreet who, humped in a doorway, massiveness of that flesh
between her shoulders somehow packaging all that was absent from
her legs, begged with a kind of bitter grimace (still knew how to curse,
'encountered on a journey to the west,' they said, 'old mannikins')
who'd marked their journey in the dream, even before they left, &
now she is here it is something else, *her* journey not theirs, he, living
out in the street, on the square, sees earth for what it is, a vast terrain,
these people here, sloped on benches or walking, these women, these
cabdrivers, passing the time of day, it pools, it shallows here, she
wants to stay, play, insist, this is not west, but east they have moved
to, the fact of it, we sit with our backs to the sea, we are facing south,
all day lightens the air before us, we are facing into the yellow earth,
toward the men of yellow corn, so the muralist had said in the
building behind them, held in the palm of the bacab of the south (it is
warm here, it is safe)—'asi pinto el mayab eterno Fernando Castro
Pacheco'

& she who must struggle to come up out of the dark, out of the west, they say is black or, coming from north, a white they do not know, of invisible bodies on visible streets, those cleaner colder roads we walk, spectral or absent, where no one lives behind the eyes that skim by: that is a kind of hell

she came up from, with owls, she came up out of the nine dark worlds of bolon tiku, & left, no not her father, lord of death, but mother—why does it change, why does the dream change it like that? He has taken his arm away from the back of the bench to light a match, his hand curved to protect the flame. I had a dream, she says, last night, so vivid I can't seem to leave it behind— Go on, he says. I was flying over a graveyard, at least I think I was flying, looking for a new coffin which was at the very end. It was out of line with the two beside it & I was supposed to straighten it but when I bent over to do that I realized I had to hang on to the middle one to give myself enough leverage & when I did my hand went through it was so rotten & I felt myself fall into the darkness of it. I was running through the dark to get home but when I got there the house was full of people, I could hear voices in the kitchen where I knew my mother was but twins of my cousin, I mean they were my cousin but twins, came into the hall to greet me, only I didn't want to see anyone so I turned to go & then I heard her voice from the kitchen call out 'I don't want to lose that one too!' I ran terrified, trying to get back here, it was if I was separate from my body, it seemed to take an extraordinary effort to get back into myself, to get back beside you & wake up.

Even telling it, terror clouds the edges of her telling & yet, now she has told it it isn't like it was, the telling fixes it in a way that wasn't felt then, a map that doesn't quite fit the terrain she was running through, doesn't take him back to that terrain the dark inhabits but like the square they are sitting in, on the same bench in the mutual day, occupies them. Not that she had meant it to take over the day, obscuring bench, trees, the balloon man, but now she can't take it back & a little embarrassed waits for him to survey it, the cigarette flaring between his fingers like a small signal. She had expected him to laugh, to make some joke, placing it thus in a waking perspective she might also enter. She has wanted him to say, as she has said to her own child on his waking, it's only a dream. But this morning he is quiet, thinking, & then he looks at her: so you went to visit your mother, he says. She hadn't thought of it as voluntary, as a 'visit,' but as a descent, perhaps she had sought out? & was that her mother? Mothers live on the earth in the day, one ascends out of the dark to mother, that's what all the stories say—but then the stories, the old stories, are always told in somebody else's language, & we don't really know. She's everybody's mother, he says, mother earth. She laughs, oh but *who* is that? *she* was definitely someone. You just

123

met her, he says.

       & the falling begins, o the horror of falling into, earth, in that we are alone—she had wanted him to pave it over, into nothing more than leaf play on paving stone, a surface she or anyone might walk across—she hadn't wanted to be alone

                                . . . hamaca? a voice says, only one hundred fifty pesos, special price for you, hennequen, very good, & the end of a pink doubleply hammock is tossed into her lap, thickly coiled end ring nestling in her skirt, look, he says, a boy, no more than a boy, nodding at her briskly, I show you, & he fans it out for her, the hennequen slivering & filming between them & separating finally into a pink & white fan extending six feet across the stones between his hand & hers. Matrimonio, he says, for two, & nods at the man beside her. She looks at Yo who laughs, who is already, in the way he sits back, dissociating himself from this exchange (she hadn't asked for—& their talk, o what about their talk?) It is to her the boy has made his advance, & though they have turned away other salesmen, the square infested with them (always a quick resentment at their fixing them so obviously as 'marks') having agreed they would not spend what money they had on a hammock, still something about the way this boy hovers, not carrying on in the usual manner, not even accompanied by a mate (as, usually, they worked the square in pairs, these hamaca men) not, obviously, out to talk them into buying but in some way waiting as he hovers there, that makes her almost want to give in—but no, she says, we don't need a hammock. Good price, he insists, but as if on the fact of it, you get nowhere else. No, she says, gracias, as he loops it toward him, deftly taking it from her lap in the last fold. Habla español? Un poco. From where you come? he asks, setting his bundle of hammocks on the stone beside their bench & sitting on it next to her. Canada. So glib, the answer to that question, but what might make sense across the divide he is trying to bridge—up north? beyond the United States? how far does his sense of north extend? She lets it rest & is surprised when he says, On-tahr-io? Of course, hamaca man. Another part of Canada, she says, the West Coast, on the sea, & points, roughly, to where she thinks the Pacific might be. He is taking a small notebook out of his back pocket, y su marido? what, perdón? hus-ban? he points, she hesitates (mi amigo? with his eyes set across the square, who is there already, butting his cigarette for a stroll, with camera, through sun & shadow, forms on benches, all that is out there she returns from, to this insistency) yes? What country? Canada too, & divining his curiosity adds, Japanese-Canadian. Ah! japonés, he scans Yo's retreating back & gestures at the book, you write for me, en Inglés? Taking the stubby pencil, she sees as he flicks through searching for a space, that it is full of words & that the writing differs, some words printed in big letters, some written phrases, some

124

Spanish, some English. I learning Inglés, he looks up seriously, people write me & I learning the words—está, la señora de On-tahr-io, she write me. The words he is pointing to say, 'take the freeway' & below that, North-south.' Freeway, he says, his finger under the word, stocky & vivid on the much handled page, hand of a farmer, broad palmed, no hamaca salesman, hands that are used to making, & suddenly, as if from some dusk, his body comes forward under the pale blue shirt, sneakers, red billed baseball cap, a young man's insistence, quiet, but humming there beside her, silent & waiting.

His eyes are on the page, as hers, & out of the force between them she asks the question, what are freeways? He audibly answers, she say me, in America, in Canada too, el camino, big trucks, much cars, go very fast very far. Of course, she thinks, & no, she thinks, you go very far here too. But how can she say that? what right has she? Me, I want to know it, he is saying, so I learning Inglés. But why? (perhaps he wants to see America like she wants to see Mexico?) He looks at her scornfully (no it is different) hamaca, he shrugs & gestures broadly across the square. Tixkokob my village, I live with my mother & father, my brothers, is small village, fifty kilómetros from Mérida. En la mañana las hamacas, he smacks the bundle he is sitting on, en la noche, las hamacas—I sell two maybe three, no good, M'entiende? not much money.

It is so clear the way he sees it, lucid as a map, but she, doubting on the far side of it, sees him lost there, the freeway of his imagination snarled in immense complications he has no vision of. It isn't only size, or only speed, what can she say? that the duplicity of map & terrain, that maps are something we are good at, countries in themselves, unreal, but perfectly believable, until one tries to set foot there & the land falls away—

Glancing around she catches sight of Yo at the heart of the zócalo facing one way & shooting down the path that leads to the eastern edge—'las lluvias olorosas' (was it promise? hope?) There is nothing she can say, he lives where he lives & will carry that with him in a way she can't foresee. And grinning sideways at her he says suddenly, first I see México, & she knows he means the capital, whence all roads lead, & which is just as far away. I learning Inglés, you teach me? tapping at the book. Si. Insistence will get him there. El Inglés es difficil, no? En mi escuela—como se dice? School? Si, school, I learning Spanish—What do you speak at home? she guesses in the same instant, Mayan? Si, Maya. Now I help my family pero en mi escuela, they have teach to me the words, to write, m'entiende? El Español no es difficil, mira: el dia, el di-a, same, m'entiende? pero en Inglés, este, de? como se deletrea de? De? (from what?) oh! day, d-a-y, she spells it out for him. Si si, es difficil. (This boy, who speaks Mayan, for whom Spanish is a second language, who

125

is trying to teach himself English phonetically, is ready to take on North America—plunked beside her on his bundle of hammocks, 'hennequen, very good.')

       Y'este, he says, tapping the book, que es r-e-y-l? Reyl? He says something in Spanish, something she doesn't understand though she gathers it's a word picked up from dos Americanos, & staring at it suddenly she gets it, rail! (of course, distance again) Si si, reyl, que es reyl? It is what a train runs along, a railroad, do you know that word? Reyl ro? please. She writes it for him in his book, sounding it out, ra-il ro(a)-d, the a, this letter, doesn't have a sound, just o, ro-d. She thinks to tell him about the sign RR, that intersection of rail & road, which after all he will know (a disappearing car) but that might complicate it for him (he who is separate, who in his Mexican version of American clothes, in his Mayan skin, comes out of some village to the east, separate & solid). No, he insists, los Americanos gave him the word & they did not say it was a train. What else could it be? rail? railing? something you hold onto? she enquires, looking around for one, sees Yo a few yards away, pointing the camera at them, & calls, what could rail mean besides railroad & railing? Ranting & railing? he laughs, an impish laugh. That's too complicated. Oh well you know I don't know English (I can't drive, he said. The package bundled up & set aside, beside him on the seat there, & separate. Wait, he would set off into that strange terrain without it, & she must stop him. Or was it her? Wait—he did not speak, or he said, they knew how to depict expression certainly, & then their iron heads rose up, scowling or grinning, out of that earth, & it was her who had brought them there—what does it mean?) Que quiere decir?—reyl? (not even a photograph can rescue them) Rule? she says, Royal? (whose rule? how get at that?) No, no (he digs away, the little man with pickaxe) something else (it was 'the power of'?)

  Oigame, he tries again, reyl, REY—L. Oh! (the pronunciation) you mean REAL? Si si, his face breaks into that smile, & they are there, they have hit it. Que es *reel*? he calls it into question (& is this real? any of it? their ground has fallen away & she is falling, how speak to that with her impoverished Spanish, his broken English?—help, it is instinct, she looks around for Yo & spots him in the centre of the square again (what is he doing?) shooting west, place of the sun's going, place of evil winds, hunger, death—this is her undertaking, this is what she must come up from. Real means actual, means, here (she slaps the bench), a thing, here (no dawning), verdad. Verdad? si? (What is the Spanish & suddenly it dawns on her, but isn't it?) En Español, real, (rey-ál) no? Ah si, si auténtico! What? I mean qué? Auténtico. Authentic! yes (he knows that word. Always it is pronunciation gets in the way, they have the same words, unrecognized, he asking her for the English she thought he hadn't known, already knowing the word

126

she hadn't recognized. But what was the question then? What is real? (reyl, some Texan speech) Auténtico he said (in the author's own hand).

Astonished, she glances up, sees Yo still at the heart of the zócalo, turned now, towards them. She wonders is he taking them or taking what stretches all around them, they only points in the whole, sees, suddenly, him seeing herself grown small with this stranger, from whom, with whom a real conversation sprouts, between them, like the trees they sit under, live among. What is your name? She asks. Manuel. Will you write it? & taking the back of the dictionary she offers, he prints

MANʋeL JEЅƱЅ

that Spanish use of Christ's name, but why not? power name, she thinks, any one might have, saviour, & connects, Manuel, Emmanuelle—wasn't it, god is with us? His hand continues to mark, abrupt strokes against the white:

PЕᶜʰ   PATꞮ

so that they form a square —these two, names from a language she doesn't recognize, printed beneath those two of heaven. Pech, mi padre, Pat, mi madre, he explains, en Inglés, you write only the name of the father, no? Pero, ademas, you are the child of your mother, m'entiende?

ground, he is saying, his or anyone's. under heaven, earth. what she had wanted to overlook, that dark, that other self she has fought up through. he comes to the edge of, telling her how it lies, horizon, what they are bound by. But where do you live? she asks, su dirección?

he writes,

DoɴMiɕiꞲio

house, but spells it, 'don,' gift, house

coɴoᴄiᴅo

known, he writes, is known (give up you know) this house you fight up through, at centre, dark, hole at the heart of the field, 'thup,' little one, where the world disappears, reaching up through the dark, through mother & up, this branching growth, gift—('in my father's house are many mansions')

When she looks from the words to his eyes they are cast down, busy under the shadow of the baseball cap with the page on which he continues to print

CALLC 21
PCPGA 130
TIXKOKob
YUC MEX

    Mi dirección, he smiles, returning them to earth, where they sit on a bench, in the heart of, handing back the book (but wait)—Allá! mi amigo! loitering several yards away, who calls, cómo le va? with a nod at her as Manuel shrugs, & slipping the notebook into a back pocket, es un vendador muy bueno, mi amigo, standing up, tipping the baseball cap at her, adios señora, hammocks slung over his shoulder, he joins his friend & fades back into the day.

                    Or their day *(El Mayab)* out in the square *(es la terra)* the men with xmas tree lights have got them down & left, the others stay, much as they have done, slumped on benches or halfturned watching passersby. Sun falls silently all around them. From a sky advanced to noon the whitewashed trunks of indian laurel bear up masses of glossy leaves against—four corners light & shadowy, these trees make of themselves, among, light bearing down *(mysteriosa y antiguo)*, she sees Yo coming toward her from across the square, she sees him walk, quick & almost light, almost disappearing into the ones he walks among, this man with whom she shares the day, whose face, alight with question, singular in that field that lights all ways—she takes her eyes from his, embarrassed by the distance—not them, they dark against its lighting—eyes slide back to, making of them in the way dark lights them, shining, showing forth what each one is, each of them in the night they also rise up from, *in which everything speaks*—well? he will say, did you learn any Mayan?—*into the . . . (silence).*

from IN THE MONTH OF HUNGRY GHOSTS

23rd   7:45 a.m.

General sweeping going on—the kabun seems to sweep the grounds each day. sounds of bamboo broom. chink of china (discreet) from kitchen. birds woke me at 7:00 with a tide of music. the old fans work well, our room cool all night tho thick with humidity.

How can I write of all this? what language, or what *structures* of language can carry this being here?

Flying in yesterday it was the size of the island that surprised me, not one hill but many, a range, all steeply wooded, overgrown. & Georgetown itself white in the sun, highrise crested now, sprawling. We came down from such a high altitude so fast the pain in my ears brought tears: the cost of re-entry? into the past?

Saturday the 24th

I have too much energy for this life, its do-nothing style—no real work to use storedup food energy. Always eating here: breakfast, lunch, dinner with tea (a meal in itself) in between. Then everyone goes to bed at 10:30. I want to get out, see the life not visible from these confines of a wellrun household. But how do it on my own? Even last night's walk with Pam down Jalan MacAllister brought us a car full of young men keeping pace with us asking if we want a ride, etc. & today Idris warns us as he lets us off for shopping alone to hang onto our purses. Tonight I have to ask Ah Yow to unlock the back door to let me in because I went out to record the chorus of frogs down the road after the house had been locked (they lock us in when they go off duty—a sealed fortress).

I'm finding out more about the taboos I was raised with, the unspoken confines of behaviour, than I am about Penang. Still, that's useful— it makes me see the root of my fears: either I obey the limitations & play safe, stay ignorant, or else I go off limits, play with "danger" & suffer the price of experience, wch is mostly unconscious anxiety that all the dire things prophesied will happen!

Saw a watersnake today in the brook I'd planned to wade down, see
where it goes—about 3 ft long, striped in bands of brown & gold
on black, coiling & uncoiling along the muddy edges of the stream
rushing thick & fast with yesterday's rainy torrents. Snake again
signals offlimits, danger to me. I can't get past the snakes in my life.

Went to market this morning with Ah Yow—lots of fish: catfish,
red snapper, even shark, plus blue crabs, various types of prawns &
shrimp, hermit crabs (brilliantly orange & black), squid too. Bought
starfruit (yellow & ridged so that the green end forms a star),
lonyons (small brown berrylike balls with flesh like rambitans & a
black pip, very fragrant, delicate), a big avocado, more mangosteens
(memory fruit, those hard black or brown rinds, redstaining flesh
inside, inedible, then in the centre soft white segments, delicious,
containing the seeds.) Little bananas here too (pisang mas), very sweet.
Plus durians & some other brown fruit about the size of Yucatan
papayas. Papayas here grow in the garden (along with purple & white
eggplants & orchids), are large & deep orange inside like the mameys.

Another swim this p.m., all of us in the sea this time, its muddy brown
waves lifting us onto coarse shale above sand where the surf comes in.
No jellyfish yet, tho Dad told us not to touch the slimy bottom further
out because ikan sembilan with poison spines lurk there. Pam & I
swim lengths of the pool for energy, but it's the salt of the sea revives
me, or memory, some further dimension. Stood in the clubhouse after
with an ayer limau (fresh limejuice & water) & watched the sea
breaking on the sand & rocks below, the foamy edge of wave curling
around the rock, soaking into sand as it withdraws drawing lines
immediately effaced, & the long recession of the wave only to be
thrown up again & again, reminded me of some, the same, watching
long ago. Must get out to the lighthouse at Muka Head.

crossing by

yellow   blue
                 to
Butter   George
worth   town
              ferry—

Pulau Pinang Pulau Jerejek Pulau Rimau

    & the light plays
        surface

Pulau blue distance leper
    haze, the Straits

of Malacca, your grandmother

        silver rack for toast
        for tennis, & the
        gardens of night-blooming
        kengwah
                    orchids, once
        every five years, the place

        "we see with alien eyes"
        "we walk with alien feet"

lifts/
            no rickshas now but 'teksis'
        & K. Tinderoomy found
        in the railroad yard
        his hand, his right leg severed

Butterworth a name

        "we commit
            to memory"

a life not of our own
        making

131

mem sahib

"mistress
of her own
house"

loved
mah mee, ordered
chicken for dinner
eased
deaths & small
wounds, cure-all,
any sepsis, except
her own

still played, gaily
mummy, mah jong, didn't
know what to "do"
(it mattered
apart from the children's
small world to move into

& lost, finally, found off-
center, *mata*, her unruly
self
unloved, locked
up in a picture, trembling
under the mask

mata hari, sun
sun through all her rooms she
closed the curtains on

from UNCOLLECTED POEMS

At Birch Bay
            for Roy
                  (thanks to Charles Olson)

black, crow, leap up   fall, flap nervous wings against a steep
invisible. bank,   against wind flutters, settle,   has none of the
sweep & glide these gulls have   open to this incessant
oncoming tide   waves & foam   wind
                              Crow, rise &
(drop something   rise & (drop,   flutter,   in to his own stress
landing against this wind, over & over.   Cracking shells, having
learned this from the gulls?
                        thru time, in the rising
wind last night I dreamt, & see, now, like the crow what it is I
learn from you
                  walking
                        walking the night as moon, moves out of
cancer, out of sea & moon pre-eminent, walking the long. tiderow-
beach. alone: white shells, white backs of gulls on the further
strand,   lift,   onto the air, clapping wings at their
re-entry into the element,   birds,   know wind changes
fast as the moon, how tide makes sand disappear, no place to be
except the turbulent face of sea itself incessant. . .
                              It was you who
entered my dream, entered me,   in the rising wind last night, in love
in the wash of opening seas we come together in : something about a
newborn you saw (rise & drop, rise &) drop   a long life line down
thru all these threshing seas, these birds, like refugees, are resting in
cloud earth sky sensorium   outside my dream, outside our dream—"ends &
boundaries," or "'space-activities' in, Creation." Within which, this
marvellous "Animate" you teach me, along with the sweep & glide these
gulls possess   this (shell) their & our   one & only   world.

                                          4/75

New Moon

> *for Roy*

A windowpane fingernail moon last night, coming into the dark room for something
outside light, where I'd left him   in the bath   having clipt tiny fingernails all
over the blue carpet—all over the blue so black stars shine   moon mostly a
finger of light appears at the crack of the door, dark, dark, circle a child
sits arm around knees—listens to their voices in the other room, promise
time holds, or light (see to the full like some pencil mark in the night sky
so faint it is the reverse of night) imagining the other side of where he sits
hugging himself in a shoe or moon, in a funny clog he sails off in, wishing. . .

briars, wishing a gate, a way *into* what remains dark for you, the
nave of an abandoned church like the belly of some whale you call me on the
phone in full daylight full of the excitement of.   This is a ship beached in
quiet halfway up a hill overlooking the sea.   This is the architrave of
sleep, "reaching 25 feet up," into invisible light on the other side of dream.
"I've found the place I want to live in"
(briar rose)

& does it sleep
at night on an empty road? do you?   Nothing sleeps, not even that briar which buds
inside you, waiting spellbound for the door to open, your door, your hand on it.

Here, I have just finished planting beans & marigolds, those flowers of the sun.
New moon, our neighbour said, I been waiting all month for this, new moon & moon
in taurus, figure you can't get more earthy than that.   Here is an architecture
of gardens, a block whose visible fences hide, under the night, the invisible
sympathy of seeds & moon.   The same you, across a sea, wake under, walk in my
imagining that white expanse of beach, dark ribs, white whale or white reflected
walls this moon a door we can't afford to look at, opens, in reverse, onto a
brilliant terrain love lives inside of, dwarfed by a rising earth, its changes.

5/75

White Lunch, not

              "white only" anymore, marble, & their closed faces, stiff
aprons. now chinese-run, now frequented by all manner of facts, colours
keep their bright appointment with the grey outside, while fictional suns
yellow & orange paper lantern (holes in the dark light slices from

                "Cut me a piece of that nice pie——"

                                    will you?
signed by the ones outside, in grey anonymous i come in from, i sit
drawn in under my wooden solitary roof, my numbered booth, & next

                                        someone
craning pale eyes from a face long in bone, long upper lip almost gone

                "You're not going now?"

gets up weight on one leg carefully pulling the other from under the
table as he pulls the cane

                "You know where I went last night?"

                              I distinct, I went, I
want had some place to go against the passing, windows of buses passing
windows of White Lunch under

                "You know where"

                            as glimpsed in passing, passed
us by you know he said, end of the world it yawns where to go, on gold
in time reflects, the duration of a coffee cup he picks up wipes the
table clean

                "You're going now?"

                "Yep."

                        plastic of one green lantern one's
attention left unlit.

                          10/78

seeing your world from the outside

                                        outside night, light
absence is whirling down.   down the order of night,   not upside,   out—
alleyways, all ways the walls say no.

                              standing inside your world is
full of holes   floating   doors: "a scream is an appraisal."   you.
apprised of what we see are messages off walls.

                                        & let me read
the black tint under your eyes from banging your head all night, against
the wall of your own want.   "salud! ladies of the night."   who do not
win *(Express yourself)*

                              Do Not phone.   Do Not move on to Go.

this game is rigged. because somebody has to be at the bottom, lottery system,
lots have to be at the bottom so somebody else comes out on top.   because
everybody wants.   & chance is the midnight bus with the winning number: will it
stop where you stop? is this the right spot? is this a stop at all?   stop.

the night is full of losers & empty buses, palisades of light adrift. nosed in
to the curb, some slight collision, lights still on, sits under neon, nothing
left to lose.   black are the scrawls of want on the walls that do not see us
("annie was here") to be lost ("take me home") in want, o baby, "will you still
feed me? will you still need me?"

black & white. & you. standing inside your world are photographing doors or
holes in the wall night pours thru.   "a scream is an appraisal."   you. a scream
is a refusal.   we.   refuse to keep in all that silence pressing thru the walls
o women, women who write

                    "because the night belongs to us"

                              11/78

Vacant, Lots

       of vacant lots vegetation fills: dandelion, tansy in tall
spokes, small clover only those close to the ground will see. in seedy
grasses waving off sandhill lots,   they weave, waving a bottle, hey!
come on over. sunstruck, drowsy & raucous, sun fuming the wine in
their heads. vacant over sidewalk, weaving up against telephone
poles. . . can't do it, man. i'm a good man,   or. my name is mud. . .

no wires over vacant lots. no connection calling them back. home
this moment, these small flowers, this much satupon mud worn into
backsides of hills they view the city from, its increment of meaning
every hoarding, every passing bus leaks, *non-sense*, a verbal
inflation that "standardizes the value of words"

                       shut up, shut up
he yells, into the open air signs fill, everywhere. 'else is better,'
they say. they want to fill up the vacant lot he is, a hole in the
system words won't fill. fill in the grass. full with friends
camped in a ring around a bottle—on vacation we say (see vacant,
see empty of work)—empty (pay, pay). & a fight erupts. someone
stoned is left alone. vacant,   we say of eyes deprived of sense
(our sense), except for nightmare: always someone climbing on somebody
else's neck,   for a bit more air. always these holes in ourselves or
where we are.
       battered & bleeding. so few words, worry beads in the
mouth, accrue value,   being tongued over & over: go fuck yourself, or.
there's a friend (in need).

hey he sez, stopping me by the liquor store, i think what for? small
change?   you better vote NDP or, lifting his cast, i'll club you over
the head. & the grin runs somewhere between me & his buddies who rock
back on their heels & applaud.
             votes get cast, silently in vacant
lots the terms run free. dying into the grass. wild not free, these men
kill the system in themselves, themselves ghosts of the open air.

                      3/79

light writes

in & out your window, woman with the trees in your face, with the sea,
fed by the mountains you said, not by the city, burning, frames the
people of this city walk through, out your window into what looks
out at what looks back, is caught up, catches, light inside their
black slow fire i'm eaten up, i'm burning, you a flesh or dreaming
i am not, a tongue to lick alight the dark your images project,
eyes looking out of darkness in that head. . .

2/79

Listen

He was reading to her, standing on the other side of the kitchen counter
where she was making salad for supper, tender orange carrot in hand
almost transparent at its tip, slender, & she was wondering where such
carrots came from in winter. He was standing in the light reading to
her from a book he was holding, her son behind him at the table where
the amber light streamed from under its glass shade bought, she had, for
its warm colour midwinter, tho he had called it a cheap imitation of the
real thing. Under it, her son was drawing red Flash & blue Superman
into a comic he was making, painstakingly having stapled the pages
together & now with his small & definite hand trying to draw exact
images of D.C. Superstars & Marvel heroes none of them had ever seen
except in coloured ink. But he was reading to her about loss, excited,
because someone had named it at last, was naming even as he read it,
the shape of what he felt to be his own, recognized at last in words
coming at him from the page, coming to her through his emphatic
& stirred voice stumbling over the rough edges of words that weren't
his, even as he was embracing them. Lost, how dancing had lost touch
with the ring dance which was a collective celebration——she was
standing with the grater in one hand, carrot in the other, wondering
if the grating sound would disturb him. She wanted to hear what had
stirred him. She wanted to continue the movement of making salad
which, in the light & the Lowenbrau they shared, was for once coming
so easily, almost was spring stirring round the corner of the house in a
rhythm of rain outside she was moving in, barely knowing, except for
the wetness of walking home——hand in hand, he was saying, a great
circle like the circle of the seasons, where now people barely touch
each other, or at least with the waltz they used to dance in couples &
then with rock apart but *to* each other, whereas now, he caught her
eye, the dances we've been to you can see people dancing alone,
completely alone with the sound.
       Lifting the carrot to the grater, pressing,
watching flakes of carrot fall to the board, she felt accused in some
obscure way, wanted to object, thought up an obscure argument about
quadrilles being collective in ballrooms where all the guests were
invited, their places in the collectivity known & symbolized by their
places in the dance. But now, & she recalled the new year's eve party
they'd been to, almost a hundred people, strangers, come, or people
don't know each other in a city the way they do in a village, but it
wasn't really that, or that only glanced off what the book was saying
about husbandry & caring for the soil. The whole carrot was shrinking
into a thousand orange flakes heaped & scattered at once, the whole
carrot with its almost transparent sides shining in the light, had ground
down to a stump her fingers clutched close to the jagged edges of tin,

she saw her fingers grating, saw blood flying like carrot flakes, wondered why she imagined blood as part of the salad . . .

Listen, he was saying, this is where he's really got it. And he read a long passage about their imprisonment in marriage, all the married ones with that impossible ideal of confining love to one—"one cannot love a particular woman unless one loves womankind," he read. Listen, he said, & he read her a passage about the ring dance, about the participation of couples in the one great celebration, the "amorous feast that joins them to all living things." He means fertility, she said, thinking, oh no, oh back to that, woman's one true function. He means fertility of the earth, he said, he means our lives aware of seasonal growth & drawing nourishment from that, instead of material acquisition & exploitation. Listen, & he read a passage about sexual capitalism, about the crazy images of romance that fill people's heads, & sexual "freedom" & "skill" & the "me-generation" on all the racks of all the supermarket stores.

Using her palms like two halves of a split spoon, she scooped up the heap of carrot flakes & set them onto a bed of lettuce, dark, because it was romaine, torn into pieces in the wooden bowl with other green things. Dance. In & out. She watched the orange flakes, glistening again in a skin of oil, dance in & out among the green she tossed with real spoons, each dipping into the dark that lay at the heart of, what, *their* hearts, they had, the other night, sunk into bed at the end of the party, drunk & floating, their laughter moving in memory through the night as they lay wrapt in the warmth of what everyone had said & how they moved away & toward each other & loved in very obscure ways. & they had made love to everyone in each other, & *to* each other, falling thru & away from each other. Listen, she said, as the rain came up & she set the salad on the wooden table underneath the lamp.

3/79

140

Bibiography

Books

Frames of a Story (Toronto, Ryerson, 1968)
leaf leaf/s (Los Angeles, Black Sparrow, 1968)
Rings (Vancouver, Georgia Straight Writing Supplement, 1971)
Vancouver Poems (Toronto, Coach House Press, 1972)
Steveston (Vancouver, Talonbooks, 1974)
Our Lives (Carrboro, Truck Press, 1975)
Steveston Recollected: A Japanese Canadian History (Victoria, B.C. Provincial Archives, 1975)
The Story, She Said (Vancouver, B.C. Monthly, 1977)
Zócalo (Toronto, Coach House Press, 1977)
Opening Doors: Vancouver's East End (Victoria, B.C. Provincial Archives, 1979)
Our Lives (Lantzville, Oolichan Books, 1980)
What Matters: Writing 1968-70 (Toronto, Coach House Press, 1980). In press.

Selected Critical Bibliography

Douglas Barbour, "The Phenomenological I: Daphne Marlatt's *Steveston*," in Diane Bessai and David Jackel, eds., *Figures in a Ground: Canadian Essays on Modern Literature Collected in Honour of Sheila Watson* (Saskatoon, Western Producer Prairie Books, 1978).

George Bowering, Review of *Vancouver Poems* in "Lines on the Grid," *Open Letter*, 2nd Series, No. 8, Summer, 1974, pp. 94-99.

Victor Coleman, Review of *Rings* in *Open Letter*, 2nd Series, No. 1, Winter, 1971/72, pp. 78-80.

Frank Davey, "Daphne Marlatt," in *From There to Here* (Erin, Press Porcépic, 1974), pp. 193-197.

Fielding Dawson, "A Psychic Hammer," in *Open Letter*, 3rd Series, No. 7, Summer, 1977, pp. 108-110.

Robert Lecker, "Daphne Marlatt's Poetry," in *Canadian Literature*, No. 76, Spring, 1978, pp. 56-67.

John Bentley Mays, "Ariadne: Prolegomenon to the Poetry of Daphne Marlatt," in *Open Letter*, 3rd Series, No. 3, Fall, 1975, pp. 5-33.

Jack Silver, "Moving into Winter: A Study of Daphne Marlatt's *Our Lives*," in *Open Letter*, 3rd Series, No. 8, Spring, 1978, pp. 89-103.

Ed Varney, Review of *Vancouver Poems* in *West Coast Review*, Vol. 10, No. 2, October, 1975, pp. 72-73.

Interviews

David Arnason, Dennis Cooley and Robert Enright, "There's This and This Connection," in *CVII*, Vol. 3, No. 1, Spring, 1977, pp. 28-33.
George Bowering, "Given This Body," in *Open Letter*, 4th Series, No. 3, Spring, 1979, pp. 32-88.